THE EXTRA SCOOP

THE EXTRA SCOOP
Rediscover the Art of Great Customer Service

JOHN MAMON
Foreword by Verne Harnish

***BOOK*LOGIX**

Alpharetta, GA

Although the author and publisher have made every effort to ensure that the information in this book was correct at the time of first publication, the author and publisher do not assume and hereby disclaim any liability to any party for any loss, damage, or disruption caused by errors or omissions, whether such errors or omissions result from negligence, accident, or any other cause.

ISBN: 978-1-61005-889-6

Library of Congress Control Number: 2017905067

10 9 8 7 6 5 4 3 2   0 4 2 4 1 7

Printed in the United States of America

⊗ This paper meets the requirements of ANSI/NISO Z39.48-1992 (Permanence of Paper)

This book is dedicated to the memory of Pop, my grandfather, whose impact on my life becomes clearer and more apparent upon the examination of its various aspects. I hope and endeavor to leave behind an imprint of similar kind and manner for my wife, children, grandchildren, extended family, and all the lives I touch professionally.

I surely hope that through me, Pop makes an impact on you too as you read *The Extra Scoop*.

CONTENTS

FOREWORD

Many of us strive daily to make our businesses the best they can be. We work on communication, growth, and teamwork. What can get lost in that daily effort is the purpose of why we do it all, and that is our Customers.

Customer loyalty seems more and more fleeting, but perhaps we are the authors of that fate. Perhaps we have taken the service we deliver to our Customers for granted. While we strive to make better products and build our companies, we sometimes leave to chance the critical and sometimes only opportunity to share with our Customers just who we are as an organization, failing to let them know just how important they are to our very existence during a Customer Service transaction.

As one of my dedicated practitioners, John Mamon understands what it takes to grow a business. In *The Extra Scoop*, John does a masterful job of mixing stories, experience, and a clear Customer-oriented perspective to drive home key points and solutions that every business needs to reach new levels. John's focus on the Customer experience is evident throughout the book and brings to life the need for each of us to adopt the same. If you walk away from this book without adopting at least one idea, you have missed the whole point.

Enjoy reading *The Extra Scoop*, and keep your highlighter handy.

—Verne Harnish
Founder of Entrepreneurs' Organization
Founder and CEO of Gazelles
and Award-Winning Author of Scaling Up

ACKNOWLEDGMENTS

This book may not have ever happened without the support of a number of special people. I have what has to be one of the most supportive wives ever. Thank you, Christine, for always unconditionally believing in whatever it is I am doing, for leaving little notes of encouragement in places I will find them just when I need them, and for sharing your life's journey with me. My daughters are also supportive in that they accept it as normal that I disappear into my downstairs office for hours on end, perhaps not yet realizing the "all in" mindset of "Big D." Thank you, Samantha and Alexis.

I would next like to thank Tony Trowbridge, Renee Kennison, Bonnie Mauldin, and Rebecca Chang for their contributions not only to this book, but to both my personal and professional lives. Each of you, in your own unique way, is special to me and I am grateful beyond words for you.

Thank you, Verne Harnish, for your contributions herein and for inspiring me to set my writing wheels in motion. I am also thankful to you for taking the time to help shape not only my professional mindset, but those of thousands of other business owners through your organizations, books, sessions, and newsletters. Keep scaling, indeed.

To Chase Carey, thank you for giving me the final push I needed to make this book happen, for all of your guidance, and certainly for your contributions to the final product. This book would not be what it is without your encouragement and reinforcement, especially in the early stages. Thank you for all you have done for me. If nothing else, I have gained a friend and close colleague in you through this process.

PART I

Whatever Happened to Good, Old-Fashioned Customer Service?

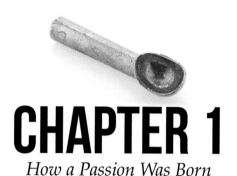

CHAPTER 1
How a Passion Was Born

As it turns out, I have a keen awareness (bordering on hyper-sensitivity) to the interaction between Customers and providers. Some of this was born from my own professional career in various roles serving my Customers, from my early teen years as a waiter to my current entrepreneurial mission of providing a great Customer experience through IT support and related cloud services (a.k.a. managed services). Early in this journey, I was employed by one of the top IT service providers in the western New York area.

I was a pretty good network engineer, so after just a short while, I found myself working with the account managers on existing Customers in presales design. It was one of those account managers who pulled me aside one day when she recognized the anxiety I was experiencing from wanting to do a really good job for a Customer and not really being sure exactly what that looked like. Here is the short version:

She said, "John, let's say you are walking down the street and want ice cream. You stop at a corner stand and ask for a cone. The guy hands you a cone without so much as a grunt and you pay him and go on your way. The next day, you want ice cream again, except this time you go to a different stand farther down the street and the man greets you with a smile and asks how your day is going. He shares a funny story while he makes your cone, and then hands it to you. You note the fact that he has placed an **Extra Scoop** of ice cream on your cone as he says, 'Thank you for coming to my stand! I hope you have a great day and that I will see you again.' "

The now obvious question followed: "The next time you want ice cream, which stand will you visit?"

Naturally, I said, "The guy who was so nice and gave me the Extra Scoop."

With a satisfied smile on her face, she replied, "That's all you have to worry about, John. Always give the Customer an Extra Scoop."

I have benefitted from that great advice throughout my career, and unbeknownst to either of us at the time, the seed was sown for what was to become my passion for Customer Service. It only made sense that it became the theme for my book.

The rest of my Customer Service "superpower" (as I like think of it) is most certainly rooted in my very own experience as an actual Customer. In the not-too-distant past, I found myself suffering from a rash of poor Customer Service experiences, the extent of which pushed me over a proverbial edge. At the end of a particularly frustrating experience, I sat staring off into space, literally astonished at what had been happening to me. I was struggling to comprehend how these organizations could deliver such poor experiences with consistency! In a brief moment of self-reflection, I wondered if perhaps my expectations were too high; maybe I was simply unreasonable in thinking that by becoming someone's Customer, I was somehow entitled to a good experience (insert dramatic pause). Like you probably just imagined, the sound of a needle being ripped off a record then screeched in my head. The notion that such expectations are unreasonable is of course preposterous, and my good sense kicked in soon thereafter, providing me the epiphany and necessary resolve to write this book.

THE EPIPHANY

The epiphany: Poor Customer Service is all too common and many of us are conditioned to expect it. In fact, we are so used to a poor experience that we are blown away when we actually have a good one. That, my friends, is a very bad trend. Allow me to illustrate.

I had the unfortunate need to call in to my insurance agent one weekend. As it turned out, the office was closed and a prompt let me know that my call was being automatically transferred to their call center. I sighed out loud, figuring this was going to be one of those bamboo-chutes-in-the-fingernails experiences. When the Customer Service representative (CSR) answered the call, she said, "Thank you for calling us today. Is this Mr. Mamon?" I replied in the affirmative and she continued, "Thank you, Mr. Mamon. Before we get started, I just want to take a moment to tell you how much we appreciate you being a Customer for so many years. It's my pleasure to serve you today." I was caught completely off guard; here I was dreading what was sure to be a painful experience—except that it wasn't at all. This CSR was so friendly and so efficient, she practically changed my whole outlook for the day. You see, I was conditioned to expect a bad experience, but she provided me quite the opposite.

Have you seen the Nationwide Insurance commercial? (Go to YouTube and search for "Nationwide Insurance Commercial 2016 One Up Two Up.") For those of you who haven't, the scene starts with a married couple talking about having to call their insurance company. When they both realize that it hasn't been done, they set about coming up with any excuse and chore to avoid being the one to have to call the company. The dad knocks over folded clothes and says he has to fold the laundry. Mom allows the baby to "paint" the window with food and claims she needs to clean the windows. Dad wildly empties the vacuum bag all over the room and says he must vacuum. You get the idea. It is a brilliant and hilarious commercial, but at the same time it is a sad commentary on Customer Service because, as this commercial clearly demonstrates, we are conditioned to expect a poor experience. All this reluctance to deal with Customer Service departments/people is well earned. Fortunately, the solutions are dead-to-rights simple which, for those of you pre-disposed to taking action, gives you the opportunity to exceed expectations and really shine.

If I accomplish anything in this book, I hope it is to illuminate for the audience that you must take a good, hard look at the experience you are providing your Customers when it comes to service. Assume nothing. Do not delude yourself that the Customer Service your company provides is adequate; adequate isn't good enough, anyway. Be proactive and start looking at it right now— you might be surprised at what you learn.

I wish I could tell you that you should keep reading because there is a magic method to providing good Customer Service. I wish I could tell you that I was the Thomas Edison of "The Sure-fire Customer Service Delivery Tool" or some other creation that was paradigm shifting and earth shattering. *The truth is that providing good Customer Service is very simple and rooted in strong, old-fashioned values.* That truth makes it more depressing that good Customer Service is terribly hard to find.

PERSONAL CORE VALUES

"All in or not in" is one of my personal core values (or some might suggest it to be a disturbing obsessive tendency—thank you, Christine). It means that if I am going to do something, I am going to give it all of my heart, body, mind, and soul. If I cannot do that, then I am not going to do it at all. By way of example, I decided at one point that I wanted to take my enjoyment of bowling to a new level. My modest goals: participating in a regional professional tour event AND not coming in last place. Before it was over, I was practicing five days a week—two with a personal coach—and had nine different bowling balls for various lane conditions and shot types. I was all in. I did all of this while working full time. You may not be surprised to learn that I did ultimately reach my goal of participating in a professional event. I didn't even finish in last place—I finished *second* to last. A subsequent hand injury limited my ability to be all in, so I am no longer competing or training. My equipment has been collecting dust ever since, but it serves as a great reminder to me of the resolve—the concerted and wholehearted effort—one needs to accomplish any goal.

"All in" suggests that you must be 100 percent committed to any objective's success. I will spare you the cliché of the inability to be half pregnant (whoops), but the reality is you can't care about Customer Service part of the time to be good at it. You can't have only half of the people in the company interested in providing it. You can't be focused solely on net profit or sales quota or widgets produced per hour. Customer Service must be an obsession; not sometimes, not most of the time, but a true obsession. It must preoccupy every mind and intrude upon every facet of your business. It should be ingrained in the company DNA. Now that's providing an Extra Scoop.

MY LAST COMPANY

I owned another IT support company with a business partner. The number-one core value in that company was "take care of the Customer at any cost." That meant that anyone at any time could make a decision to do whatever was necessary to help the Customer without fear of reprimand, even if it broke with process. That in and of itself is very powerful. If you don't fully support your Customer Service professionals in all their decisions, what they do to help your Customer will be limited too. We will touch more on that later.

We were a very process-driven company because in the IT industry, a good process is critical to positive outcomes. Part of our process was to be ever mindful of the Customer's experience. We would always do a "lesson learned" session when a process failed to provide the Customer with the experience we intended. There's a good question in there: are you *intentional* about a positive Customer experience?

The number-one core value of my current IT company built upon that foundational "take care of the Customer . . ." mindset and now includes more than just the Customers themselves and encompasses more than just post-transaction support. We expanded beyond Customers to include every person we interact with, including our partners, vendors, employees, the person who needs help with their printer, the person who writes the checks to pay us every month, and everyone in between. They all deserve a great experience too. This value permeates and dictates everything we do and every decision we make. Want to add a new service? How does that affect the Customer experience? Changing a process? What's the impact to the Customer? Remember, you can't just look at margins, profits, and incremental sales (although you *do* have to look at them). You must look at the Customer impact too. Do you know why? (Hint: Customers = sales = profits. More on his equation later.)

In my business, bad Customer Service means you are *fired*. I treasure every Customer relationship. I am so thankful that a business owner has placed their trust in me and is paying me hard-earned money for my service that I dare not do anything but my very best to provide the best experience for them I possibly can. One wonders how some of these folks that are responsible for Customer Service at other companies got to that position. Perhaps they should be a starving entrepreneur for a period of time, thereby gaining a new appreciation for how crucial every Customer is and, by extension, every experience they deliver to them thereafter.

BELIEVE ME, THIS BOOK IS FOR YOU

If you have a business, you have Customers. If you have Customers, you serve them. If you are serving Customers, you are in the Customer Service business. So, this book is for every business owner out there, from the person with a hot-dog stand to the company providing insurance solutions to a manufacturer with many employees. I'm talking to the managers and vice presidents out there responsible for Customer Service. I am talking to the presidents and CEOs too. And I'm talking to supervisors and Customer Service reps. I'm talking to *every* stakeholder of any business that provides a service to anyone, and that means pretty much everyone. It's time to listen and listen well.

I have just a few housekeeping items to go over as we get started. The first is that you will notice that the word "Customer" is capitalized throughout the book, and that's because I want you to recognize how important Customers are to your business. I want you to revere them as royalty and thus, a customer is not just a noun; it is a title. The next item is that the stories you will find throughout the book are all true and recorded from either my own personal experiences or from interviews and shared stories of others. Names, of course, have been changed for privacy. I don't mention the name of any companies that delivered poor experiences (hey, you know who you are), but I will on occasion reference the ones that have delivered great ones.

Also, while Customer Service spans the entire life cycle of a Customer's engagement (sales, acquisition of product, etc.), you will note that most of our discussion points are around post-transaction support, though many of the principles can be applied throughout the Customer life cycle. There is also a fair amount of time spent discussing the topic of phone interactions, and it's important to remember that many of those principles can apply to face-to-face interactions.

I refer to Customer Service representatives (CSRs) throughout the book as a generic title for those people whose job it is to service the Customer. You may feel free to exchange any title you like for people in those roles. Finally, be sure to pay attention to the Extra Scoops at the end of each chapter—there's gold in them there hills.

So with that, off we go to explore "whatever happened to the Extra Scoop."

Your Chapter 1 Extra Scoop
Be obsessive about Customer Service. Know that every Customer is priceless and treat them as such.

CHAPTER 2
Whatever Happened to an Extra Scoop of Ice Cream?

Many aspects of Customer Service are going the way of the fax machine—they are headed for extinction. It wasn't all that long ago that good Customer Service was a virtuous social standard. It was the paradigm, not the exception that it seems to have become today. Somewhere along the line, attitudes began to change and with them, organizations began to view Customer Service as a necessary evil. That mindset has begotten poor service, poor reputations, and Customers who would just as soon take their business anywhere else. One study noted that 58 percent of Customers with a negative experience will never use that company again, though you can bet that they *will* buy from your competitor.[1] Here's a truth you should get comfortable with:

Poor Customer Service = Lost Customers + lost brand appeal + lost goodwill

---

[1] "The multibillion dollar cost of poor customer service." NewVoiceMedia. December 12, 2013.

Recognize that lost Customers also include potential future Customers. Poor Customer Service can paint your brand negatively or worse yet, stain it indelibly. This has a compounding effect on a company's goodwill. If you are leaking Customers, your brand appeal and goodwill are leaking out with them.

It is difficult to say with any precision when or why the decline in Customer Service began. Seemingly, there was a transition from Customer Service being a "must do" to a "have to." This may have started in the latter half of the 1980s; there was a significant recession, a lot of white-collar layoffs, and the quality of US durable goods (appliances and cars in particular) plummeted. Reactively, executives and employees turned inward, pointing out the "other" employees, managers, or executives responsible for the financial effects brought to their shores by an influx of better, cheaper foreign goods. It was impossible to keep up with inflation.

The only rule that counted was the bottom line rules. Companies began making the critical mistake of cutting corners that directly impacted Customer Service to fatten profit percentages. Ironically, this shortsighted view often had the complete opposite effect on total profit:

The cost of new Customers + lost referrals > The
cost of good Customer Service

It may seem that you will get an extra point or two of profit, but you will trade current and future revenues from lost Customers, lost referrals, and immeasurable damage to your brand. All of this ultimately adds to your cost of sales and negates the very savings you had hoped for to begin with. Still, the sentiment continues today.

Maybe it started in the "have to" attitude itself. When you are the ugly stepchild in a business, ambivalence begins to creep in and affect everything it touches. Perhaps the Customer Service archetype became less than attractive and was something you talked about only when you had to. After all, the glitz and glamour are in sales and revenue, right?

Or was it a pervasive "it's just business" mindset? Business was different and separate from our personal lives, and the rules you used in interacting with your neighbors were not to be applied at work. We went from a "we" perspective to an "us and them" perspective. As it turns out, "Us and Them" became an historic Pink Floyd song, which made for great dorm music but a lousy business mantra—a mantra that unfortunately continues to strangle many businesses today.

Maybe it is rooted in a flawed notion that sales are abundant and good Customer Service is not necessary. Thanks to the Internet, many companies have virtually no boundaries for marketing and sales, so a business's reputation doesn't necessarily impact it the way it did before when they had a much smaller sales and marketing sphere. Let's face it, word-of-mouth marketing was far more critical in the past. Audiences are now global and there will always be other buyers, so why spend the money and make the effort to be great at Customer Service? One can argue social media is far more insidious than sharing a poor experience one backyard fence at a time, but I am not sure it has the proportional impact to sales—not yet, anyway.

Another impact could be the thought process that Customer Service was only important to those other guys providing actual services, like a doctor, an accountant, or lawyer. That is not true, of course, as I have already said that if you have a business, you provide Customer Service. An added sentiment may have been that you can overcome stripped-down Customer Service with a superior product. That is also a fallacy. A quality product (or a bad one, for that matter) and providing quality Customer Service are inextricably linked in your Customer's mind. Customer Service exists before, during, and after the Customer agrees to purchase your product, superior or otherwise. If I am purchasing an appliance from you, you provide me service before the purchase (explaining the features, providing me a positive shopping environment, etc.), you provide me a service by getting the appliance to me (i.e., delivery), and you certainly provide me service post-acquisition, like providing support for when I have questions or something goes wrong.

One final theory I would share in an effort to explain the decline of good Customer Service is that as the world became "flat" (Thomas L. Friedman's *The World Is Flat* is a wonderful book on this topic), more and more organizations began to look overseas for outsourcing opportunities and readily found them. This led to myriad Customer Service challenges that haven't been solved by most. More on this later in the book.

I have found some common characteristics of organizations that have consistently poor Customer Service. One or more of these characteristics exists in such a scenario:

1) There is a lack of competition. If the Customer has few or no options, where will they go if they are unhappy? If this is your company, let me just say shame on you for taking advantage of your market position. Just know that if you continue, you will someday see a mass exodus when options inevitably become available. I can think of a couple of companies I will stop doing business with as soon as certain alternatives are available.

   i) Think I am kidding? Does anyone remember a company called Blockbuster? Yes, yes . . . the company was certainly caught flat-footed when new, technology-driven competitors arrived on the scene (i.e., Netflix), but no one can forget the fact that Blockbuster was beset by a multitude of Customer Service issues, throughout its later years at least. When new options became available, there was no stopping the masses from moving on, perhaps quite literally in spite of efforts by Blockbuster to meet new Customer demands.

2) There is a lack of Customer-related core values and focus starting at the top. Customer Service is simply not in the company DNA (yet).

Good news: both of these characteristics can be fixed. Just decide you want to.

I NEED SOME ICE CREAM

I really want to get to telling you about some Extra Scoops, but some of this historical detail is important because it implies that good Customer Service did indeed exist (and does today for select organizations) and companies were profitable (it's not tooth-fairy stuff, I promise!).

I grew up in a different time. I am not that old, mind you (unless you ask my teenage daughter), but I distinctly remember going on weekend errands with my grandfather in the early '70s. He went to the same filling station every single Saturday (that's a gas station for those who don't remember or weren't alive). As you pulled in, you could observe a handful of people literally dropping everything they were doing to come provide service to Customers at the pump. The service included opening the hood, checking the oil, topping off any low fluids, and, oh yes, pumping the gas.

My grandfather bought all of our shoes at the exact same shoe store, *every* time. As a kid, it didn't matter if they had a shoe you liked or not—that's where you were getting them. Upon arrival, we were all treated as royalty. The candy bowl came out from its hidden place under the counter for more than one choice of your favorite confection. Sodas were offered on the way to your seat. After learning what you were in the market for, the shoe parade began. Dozens of different choices were brought to your chair, and you never had to put one shoe on yourself. It seemed like we were there for hours every time we went in.

And I can remember the milk being delivered to our house in the box outside the door. The milkman always came a day earlier to find out what we needed and wrote things down in a small spiral notepad with a pencil he kept behind his ear.

Even though it was long ago and I was a little boy, I still remember the people who owned these businesses. Roy was the gas-station owner, and Louie and Stu owned and ran the shoe store. Mike visited us once per week in a green and white–panel truck for our dairy order.

I remember going to the same bakery each Saturday morning and the same pizza place every Saturday night. Even with my vivid memory of these times, I cannot recall there ever being a problem during any of those experiences. I also remember my grandfather taking me to his two jobs on the weekend. His main job was that of a manager at a chemical plant, and I will always remember how he made sure everyone stayed busy. If you weren't, it was time to paint the forklifts. You would have thought that the forklifts were brand new off the production line. They sparkled in spite of their heavy use and grimy surroundings. His other position was as night manager of an RV-sales company. He used to let me sit and listen while he showed a trailer to a prospective buyer. I can remember him always walking with a cloth hanging in his back pocket, and he would stop and polish any spot he saw while still answering any question or objection the buyer might have. I don't think he ever told a single person he couldn't "take care of that" for them. The days of seeing a cloth in a back pocket may be long gone, but how many of your employees pass by a Customer who looks lost or ignore a phone line that has been on hold forever?

There are a number of implications here that you may have already caught on to. One, Customer Service is personal. I remember the names of all of those people who took care of us. Two, good Customer Service engenders loyalty in a world where it is tough to come by, given the plethora of choices at our fingertips. Last but not least, good Customer Service requires a *concerted and wholehearted effort*. Remember, you must be all in or you're not in.

WHERE HAVE YOU GONE?

Let me ask you, whatever did happen to getting that Extra Scoop of ice cream? Most have forgotten the concept of the Extra Scoop. The Extra Scoop was born from a desire to distinguish my business from the guy on the next corner (be different), to deliver more value (be better), to garner word-of-mouth referrals (get more sales), and, oh yeah, also just to take great care of Customers (create a better experience).

Can you imagine the improvement in your company's Customer Service experience if you did this one simple thing: Put a sign above every CSRs monitor that said, "Go out of your way and be extra nice to people today. Make each person you talk to today feel extra appreciated. Let them *know* they are *special*." I know, I know. I can hear a bunch of you COOs and CFOs grumbling, but you really need to remember the value of delivering great Customer Service.

The Customer Service department is a company's best sales tools. That's right. Good Customer Service drives sales. Let me repeat: good Customer Service drives sales. Inverse to the formula provided earlier:

$$\text{Good Customer Service = New Customers +}$$
$$\text{retained Customers + brand appeal + goodwill}$$

Good Customer Service *directly* impacts repeat purchases, upselling, and the company's ability to sell at above-market prices. Delivering a better Customer experience has and always will mean that you are a better company, and it translates into more sales and more profit. You *could* often charge more for that reason alone. Remember my filling-station story, when they used to check your oil and clean your windshield? Why did they do this? Because it generated more sales. Great Customer Service generated repeat sales, and checking the oil and finding it was low resulted in the purchase of a quart of oil, an important add-on sale. In the 1950s through the 1980s, Prudential Insurance was the gold standard in insurance Customer Service. So much so, it was widely known to businesses that if they wanted Prudential health insurance for their employees, they were going to have to pay about 5 percent more. How were sales? They were not to be beaten! Businesses wanted their employees to be well taken care of and they were willing to pay for it. Customer Service is a major differentiating factor, and yet companies seem to deliver poorer and poorer experiences.

Let me share an example of what an Extra Scoop does *not* look like. I live in Metro Atlanta and, like a lot of large urban areas, we have traffic. In some parts of the day and in some directions, it just takes forever to get from here to there. One day, I had to take my trailer in for repair. There aren't a lot of trailer businesses around, as you can imagine, and the one closest to me was forty-five minutes away, well away from my office. I took it in and they told me it would be ready on Thursday. They even gave me a call the following week and told me it was ready. I moved some appointments around to get there to pick it up, drove across town, changed out of my suit in the restroom of the store, and stepped into a long line at the Customer Service counter. There were as many people behind the counter as there were people in line, yet there was only one person helping Customers. After a fifteen-minute wait in line, it was my turn. The service representative remembered me from my drop-off and called back to the shop to have my RV brought up. A smile came over his face as he hung up and looked at me, saying, "It's not ready."

So, I basically lost two hours out of my workday to find out that the trailer wasn't ready even though they told me it was. Clearly upset, I asked, "Why did you tell me it was ready?"

He chuckled, "I thought it would be. It will be two more days."

I said, "I am glad you find this humorous. I certainly do not." Credit is due in that he now at least recognized I was unhappy. Now, folks, this is not a big deal in the grand scheme of things, but the nonchalance with which this news was delivered, on top of how long I waited in line just to find out this information—well, it really irked me. Not only did I not get an Extra Scoop, I got an empty cone with my due scoop lying on the floor. This was a two-hundred-dollar repair job, and although not a budget buster to them or to me, it was the lack of acknowledgment of the mistake and value of my time that made me despise the service. Remember, I still had to do this all over again when my trailer was finally ready.

So, how could this have been an Extra Scoop experience? Something as simple as this:

> "Mr. Mamon, I am really sorry we brought you
> all the way over here for no reason and we missed

the delivery time. The first thing I am going to do is assure you we will get to working on your trailer this afternoon, and I will have Freddie drive it over to your home or business by four o'clock tomorrow afternoon. I am also going to give you a twenty-five-dollar credit on any future service. Will that be okay for you?"

Do you know what this would have cost the trailer dealer? My guess is about fifty dollars when you factor in gasoline and Freddie's time in traffic. Not a big deal. They never would have noticed the cost and they would have had a happier Customer. In fact, if they had done this for me, it would have created a much bigger impression on me than if my trailer had even been ready. By the way, their next closest competitor is miles and miles away from me. Do you remember the conditions that typically exist in a company with consistent poor service?

Let me ask you something. Isn't the Extra Scoop the right thing to do? The Extra Scoop is not necessarily about giving anything away in order to deliver good Customer Service. Rather, it is the mindset of doing whatever it takes to provide a positive experience. It is each touch point and interaction going well for the Customer. *It is delivering something the Customer is conditioned not to expect—going above and beyond.* It's behaving in a way that makes a Customer (or potential Customer) feel they matter, that they are special and important. During the sales process, this might be giving the buyer a relaxing decision environment and then rewarding them after a positive decision (like sending cookies or providing a gift card for their next visit). Once they have become a Customer, it might be providing a friendly delivery driver that's on time and puts on booties over his shoes so as to not get your carpet dirty. When I need support sometime down the road, an

Extra Scoop could be as simple as providing me a frustration-free interaction. Frustration free—now there's a novel idea!

In the simplest terms, the Extra Scoop is about exceeding expectations for the Customer by providing an excellent experience (in your desire to be "Extra-Scoop Certified," you don't leave expectations to chance, so we will talk about that more in a later chapter). With the Customer Service bar now so sadly low in many industries, how hard could it be to stand out in the crowd?

Your Chapter 2 Extra Scoop
To be a truly great company, you must have great Customer Service.

PART II

What Are Some
Extra Scoops?

CHAPTER 3

Whatever Happened to Good Manners?

Customer Service seems void of courtesy these days. Didn't interactions used to include words and phrases like, "Could I ask you to hold for just a moment?" "Is there anything else that I may do for you?" and of course "please," "thank you," and "you're welcome"? Sadly, it seems manners are viewed as anachronistic.

Borrowing from a Linton Weeks 2012 article for NPR, Gregory E. Smith, a psychiatrist and blogger in Augusta, Georgia, says, "Simple things that we took for granted as children no longer seem to count. Saying please and thank you, asking permission, offering unsolicited help, and following up on solutions to problems are no longer [deemed] as important."[2]

When it comes to Customer Service, I am sure some of it grew out of keeping service calls short. Starting out in a conversational tone and being polite can foster conversation that does nothing to resolve the Customer's issue and thus potentially prolongs an interaction, keeping wait times for other Customers higher. Thus, the practice of good manners is . . . inefficient?

---

[2] Weeks, Linton. "Please Read This Story, Thank You." NPR. March 14, 2012.

Like other aspects of Customer Service though, a better balance must be struck between efficiency and experience. You cannot deliver a cold, sterile, uncaring, script-driven interaction and deliver the kind of Extra Scoop experience I advocate. You should also not confuse the use of good manners with providing over-the-top kindness. The former makes a Customer feel respected and that the CSR is professional, well trained, and well intentioned; the latter can often come off as learned, scripted, even disingenuous and irritating (particularly if you haven't been able to actually solve the Customer's problem).

Remember that people are not calling to tell you that the sun is shining and everything is rosy; they are calling to tell you something is wrong, broken, not working, or they simply can't figure something out. They need help and many times they are already frustrated and/or upset. The last thing most people want to do is take time out of their life to call Customer Service. The way to instantly and positively impact an upset Customer is to treat him or her politely. It may take four or five sentences to get them there, but if your CSRs remain polite, the Customer will start to calm down and will be grateful for treating them like a good person even though they may have been wearing their crazy hat. (Come on, I know you have one. Many of us put it on the moment we pull out of our driveways!)

REMEMBER THE GOLDEN RULE?

Manners are still important, folks. "Do unto others as you would have them do unto you" should still be a guiding principle. Perhaps Dr. Tony Alessandra's "Platinum Rule" better applies to our topic of Customer Service: "Treat others the way *they* want to be treated." Whichever you prefer to subscribe to, you would be well suited to put some precious metal into your Customer Service mix, and there is a simple way to get started: strive for great entrances and exits.

> "All the world's a stage,
> And all the men and women merely players;
> They have their exits and their entrances,
> And one man in his time plays many parts."

Our good friend William Shakespeare has left us many a good quote, and his "exits and entrances" line has been used many times in many speeches, but I love it as an improvement theme for CSRs. Now, please don't read here that what happens between the entrance and exit isn't important; we will just cover that in some other chapters. With that, let's start with *entrances*.

You've no doubt experienced why first impressions are so important. A first impression sets the tone for an encounter. In a Customer Service interaction, it lets the Customer know what he or she is in store for; it speaks volumes about your organization and how important you deem the people that are the reason for its existence (your Customers). A first impression demonstrates how much you invest in selecting and nurturing the people on your front lines.

I had called in to a prospective Customer one day. Mind you, this woman probably fielded dozens of calls like mine each day, but I am here to tell you that I had an amazing interaction with her. When she answered the phone, she said in a singsong voice that could only be produced with an ear-to-ear smile on one's face, "Thank you so much for calling Company XYZ today. What can I do to help you?" Naturally (or maybe unnaturally), I pulled the phone away from my ear for a split second and stared at the receiver. I thought to myself how I would love this woman to be working for me! I put the phone back to my ear and asked her name (Helen), then said, "Helen, before I tell you the reason for my call, I want you to know that you are a real asset to your company. That was a wonderful first impression—thank you!" She thanked me for the compliment and we exchanged additional pleasantries before she eventually transferred me to her boss, who was the subject of my call to begin with. When he picked up the phone, I told him the same thing I told her. He thanked me as well and noted that he gets multiple compliments each week about her. Wouldn't you like your Customer Service department to be known this way?

A good exit is equally important. Working on a problem with a Customer is not always easy and it may not go as smoothly as you would hope. At the end of a service transaction, helping the Customer feel appreciated and that you are thankful for them can go a very long way. Here's another personal example. I had to call into my wireless carrier, and although I didn't have a problem per se, I still had something I needed help and advice with. Once my questions were answered and as we were about to terminate the call, the CSR actually asked me how my overall experience was with the carrier. Caught off guard, I stumbled out a weak "it's okay." What I most remember was how strongly she reacted when she said, "I am sorry that your experience is not great, but I hope my assistance today was a great experience for you. What else can I do to help you and make your experience a great one?"

I'm still wondering if I somehow got rerouted to Mars by mistake. I replied back that she did a great job and really helped me, but I didn't need any further assistance. In one seemingly heartfelt sentence (remember—good Customer Service is personal), that CSR changed my entire perception of the company. They went from an uncaring, money-sucking one of many to a compassionate, helpful, quality organization that I am thankful to do business with—just like that.

Now, do you think when I go to add additional phones to my account I am going to shop around and find the cheapest carrier?

There is not a single chance I am going to shop elsewhere. And who knows, maybe my carrier is five dollars or ten dollars more per phone per month (I don't know that they are), but for that kind of caring and service, I'll pay it.

One thing that I don't want to get lost here is the reality that many people making a purchase decision do so based on emotion. The only time this may not be true is in choosing what emergency room to go to when in need. However, with almost all other decisions and purchases, we do make them with emotion. If a company makes me *feel* good, I am far more willing to do business with them. This is not an inconsequential point when it comes to the sales component of our Customers = sales = profits formula. In many, many cases, it's why we buy, and that's why you should rush to ensure manners are a part of your service paradigm. The best part? It won't cost you a thing to make it happen.

It's not hard to add "happy Friday" to the beginning of a call. It's no more difficult to say "I hope you have a fantastic rest of your day" at the end. "Please" turns a demand into a request. "Thank you" acknowledges the person for helping you to help them. "You're welcome" lets them know you are happy they engaged you and you'd be happy to help them again.

Adding an Extra Scoop is easy. Wouldn't you agree?

Your Chapter 3 Extra Scoop
Remember that "please" and "thank you" can often be the most powerful words in business. They are certainly the most disarming.

CHAPTER 4

Whatever Happened to Having a Conversation?

In his book *The 7 Habits of Highly Effective People*, the great Stephen Covey said, "Seek first to understand, then be understood." What a fabulous tenet for Customer Service.

So much of Customer Service is scripted these days. In an effort to increase profits, businesses hire people with no experience or no grasp of the English language (or both), give them a week of training (or less), and put them on the front lines with what they think is magical pixie dust—a script. Customers call in, the inexperienced CSRs reach into the bowl and then sprinkle magic dust in the air, whimsically solving the Customer's problem on the spot, except it fails to do its job—a lot. Maybe the motivation is to provide a consistent experience. That would be okay if the experience was consistently good, but again, it's not.

This is a great business practice if you want your Customers to be as unsatisfied as possible, don't want repeat sales, and couldn't care less about upselling. In a recent survey by a call-center software provider, "scripted-sounding agents" was identified as a key Customer Service pain point.[3] When your Customer calls

---

[3] "Report: Consumer Boiling Points Prove Bad for Business in 2015." Marketwired. December 3, 2015.

in, does your CSR essentially wait for dead space and then read from a script? A rigid script does not provide a good experience; it *frustrates* at minimum and *insults* at maximum. Rigidly sticking to scripts projects a cold, sterile, noncaring approach, when Customer Service needs to be warm and accommodating. It communicates you are only going to do the bare minimum and hope for the best. It breeds misunderstanding. It's destructive and will alienate your Customers. Moreover, the rigid use of scripts exacerbates the lack of experience for the typical CSR, never allowing them to stretch their Customer Service chops and become better at communicating with Customers. CSRs don't feel empowered to act. A rigid script means you have predetermined what I need versus helping me get where I really need to go. My need, my support, my destination—not yours.

Well, that was a mouthful. I think you get my general thoughts on call scripts. Please allow me to straighten my tie and pull my shirt taut as we dive a little deeper.

CONTEXTUAL SCRIPTS

"Okay, okay, John," you say. "But scripts are not going away and likely never will. So what are you suggesting?" Good question. My answer is that I want you to use what I will call contextual scripts to *support* your CSRs, not to make them sound like a robotic recording. "It's hard for agents to convey empathy with the Customer when every word is preplanned," said Brandon Knight, vice president of contact-center optimization for Corvisa.[4] I couldn't have said it better myself.

Scripts do have their place, but a rigid script provides a word-for-word, inflexible experience that actually trains CSRs not to communicate and not to listen. It can be an utterly exasperating experience

---

[4] Ibid.

for a Customer. In contrast, a contextual script can be an excellent tool to help guide CSRs in the *structure* of how a call should flow. A contextual script will help in making sure that all aspects of a call are completed and information gathered, while allowing CSRs to genuinely communicate. In addition, contextual scripts are great tools to help CSRs know when they have hit specific limits in a conversation, or more specifically, limits in their ability to solve the problem. In helping them identify these limits, they can more quickly get the Customer into another channel to help get their problem solved. That equals a happier Customer and a happier CSR.

ONE RESULT OF A RIGID SCRIPT

If you have ever had to call in to a Customer Service center (really, who hasn't?), then you can probably insert your own story here. Here is one person's experience while trying to get help with a software product:

CALLER: (*Dials the number for help.*)
CSR: Hi. May I have you name please?
CALLER: Frank Smith (names are changed to protect the innocent).
CSR: May I have your phone number?
CALLER: 555-867-5309.
CSR: Can I have the product ID that you are calling about?
CALLER: 12-6789.
CSR: Do you have an extended warranty?
CALLER: No.
CSR: When was the product purchased?
CALLER: About three months ago.
CSR: Where was it purchased from?
CALLER: Ummmm . . .
CSR: Do you have the receipt?

CALLER: Uhhh . . .

CSR: Shoe size, please . . .

> **We interrupt this program to bring you a public service announcement. It is unreasonable to ask a million questions before you even ask how you might help the Customer.

CSR: What is the nature of the problem?

CALLER: Well, I have three different questions about the product.

CSR: How long has the problem been happening?

CALLER: Well, as I said, it is a few questions.

CSR: What is your question?

CALLER: Well, the first question is that I am getting a license error even though I was assured that I was buying the right license.

CSR: I see. Okay, sir. Your incident number is 98-76543. You have reached the wrong department for the help you need. In the future, you must call 555-123-4567. Stand by and I will transfer you.

CALLER: Wait! That is the number I called!

CSR: I am not sure how you got here then, sir, but I will transfer you now.

CALLER: Hold on! Can you give me the incident number again? I wasn't prepared to write anything down.

CSR: 98-76543. I am transferring you now. Before I do, is there anything else I can help you with today?

> **We interrupt this program to bring you a public service announcement. It is unreasonable to ask if you can help with anything else when you haven't helped with anything at all.

CALLER: Ummm . . . I guess not. (*Call is transferred.*)

CSR 2: Hi, may I have your name, please?

CALLER: Frank Smith. I have an incident number.

CSR 2: Umm. I am sorry, sir. I have no way to reference an incident number from another department.

**We interrupt this program to bring you a public service announcement. It is *unacceptable* to not be able to reference caller/incident information between CSRs/departments. Why would you bother to give them a reference number if it does no good?

I think you get the idea. Can you feel the frustration building for the caller? When you see it on paper, does it not look absurd? The CSR is reading a line-by-line script, and a poor one at that. The experience is a setup for failure for everyone involved.

Let's take a look at what a contextual script might look like. Keep in mind that this is not meant to be an exhaustive example and that there may be certain deviations from organization to organization, but each script should have these same basic ingredients.

- Module One – Provide a Great Entrance
  * Exchange pleasantries.
  * Listen to the issue sympathetically.
  * Repeat the issue back to the Customer.
  * Make sure they are in the right place!
  * Attain Customer-specific data (name, number, account information, product ID, etc.).
  * Record all information in the service system.
  * Assure the Customer that you are on their side and you will stick with them until someone else is on the phone to help them.
- Module Two – Work to Solve the Problem
  * Determine effort Customer has already made to solve the issue.
  * Walk the Customer through any troubleshooting steps that are appropriate. Make sure that the CSR is patient and understanding through the process.

* Test any perceived solution and be *sure* the Customer agrees it is solved.
* If the problem persists, go to the "Escalation" module.
* Go to the "Exit" module.
* Module Three – Escalation
    * Determine appropriate team/CSR for escalation.
    * Remind the Customer you are going to stick with them until they are in another set of good hands (warm handoff).
    * Provide ALL the information to the new CSR for the Customer. Don't make them do it!
    * Do not make them wait in a hold queue again.
* Module Four – Provide a Great Exit
    * Be certain the Customer is completely satisfied.
    * Determine if there are any other issues that you can help the Customer with.
    * Thank them for allowing you to take care of their problem.
    * Ask them to honestly tell you where the process can be improved.
    * Provide them with the case number and phone number in the event they have any further issues.
    * Ask the Customer if they are aware of the latest model being released or upgrades available to the service/product they have.
    * Make them feel great as you say goodbye.

You will also need some kind of "Supervisor" module to handle situations where a person is irate or unreasonable, or if the situation just breaks down and comes off the rails. You should have a "Sales" module that helps a CSR through a process of sales/upselling once the call is completed satisfactorily and the Customer expresses an interest.

Here's the thing that I hope you are gleaning from this. Your CSRs must be trained and allowed to work within the context of the conversation and not robotically read line for line. Rigidity limits your CSRs' ability to provide a good experience.

CSRs need to hear what the Customer's problem is as effectively and as humanly as possible. They should echo back the issue so it is clear everyone is on the same page. Once a Customer knows that you understand what they need, they feel like they have a pretty good chance at getting it and then their confidence in having a good outcome/experience increases. "Mr. Customer, I hear you. It sounds like you are concerned/frustrated/lost about our product/service. I promise you I am going to do everything within my power to resolve this for you and have you be a very pleased Customer. Do you mind if I ask you a few questions so I can get our call documented and I can verify a few things? It will only take a moment." I feel better already!

KEY SCRIPT-RELATED POINTS

1) Listen actively and repeat the problem back. Most companies would do a multitude better by simply executing the phrase "let me repeat that back to you."
2) Make sure your CSRs are able to provide feedback on the script structure and make changes where necessary.
3) Make sure the CSRs have a repository to record the Customer feedback given in the "Exit" and that

this feedback is reviewed regularly by supervisors and managers.

4) Contact both happy and unhappy Customers to help you improve the Customer experience.

5) Make sure it is *crystal clear* when a CSR *must* bring in a supervisor to assist. This should not and cannot be viewed as a failure on the CSR's part. This action should be *encouraged*!

6) Make your supervisors/managers spend a certain amount of time each week on your front lines as CSRs. If your supervisors and managers are good at what they do, they will learn quickly what is not working and will have the authority to fix it or add additional training for the CSRs.

7) When appropriate, offer the Customer an opportunity to purchase something—even if it's at a discount due to their issue.

8) Always offer to handle things for the Customer. Don't make them repeat a bunch of information or call back in to a new line, and don't abandon them in the process of getting them to the right place.

9) Always ask for honest feedback and record it as part of your call process.

10) Instruct CSRs to *smile through the phone.*

11) Make sure CSRs don't get hung up on solving every problem. Know when to escalate.

On this last point, I want to share a story from a very good friend of mine. He called in to a wireless communication company for support. Personally, I have known this company to have very good support, as I am a Customer of theirs as well. In this particular case, though, my friend struggled with a CSR for over forty minutes and was getting nowhere. He asked to be transferred to a higher-level tech more than once, but the CSR seemed to ignore that request. He was so frustrated that he even said he would *pay* extra to speak to someone else if that is what it took. He just wanted the problem solved. Finally, after another twenty minutes of wrestling with the problem, the CSR escalated the issue and got another technician on the phone. The problem was solved within five minutes once the right person was on the call to handle the problem. You have been there, right?

Let's wrap up with an example of a great Customer Service call. This true story happens to be one provided by my wife, Christine, who is, unfortunately for her, the designated deal-with-Customer-support adult in our house. Let me tell you, she has some "doozies" for stories (or "Deusies" for those that recall the origination of the term), which was what made this interaction she had with Apple stand out so greatly. Let's face it, folks, Apple is not one of the largest companies in the world for no reason, and I assert to you that it's not only because they produce great technologies, it is because they provide a *great* Customer experience. As you read the story, see if you can pick out some of the things they did to ensure she had a great experience.

One day, she had difficulty uploading files to an external device from her AirBook. She had not had the problem previously, so she wasn't really sure what to do and decided to call Apple technical support. She used Google to find out how to contact them and easily found her way to a live-chat support feature. On the chat, the CSR conveyed great kindness (not an easy task through a chat service) and thanked her for contacting them. She was taken aback by how he assured her that he was going to help her solve this issue and gave her a case number.

At this point, she had a problem with our home Internet connection (don't you love Murphy's Law?) and the chat session was disconnected. When the Internet service was restored, she launched a new chat session and a new person connected. She relayed the case number and lo and behold, the new CSR knew who she was and what challenge she was facing. The new CSR asked for a few more details, and then again assured her that she would help her or get her to the right person who could.

As it turned out, she did need to be transferred and that determination was made quickly. Christine was really worried about being transferred to someone else because she had been treated so well by the first two CSRs. She just assumed there was no way she would be lucky enough to get to someone else like them. Her concerns were instantly erased when she was transferred to CSR 3, who came onto the chat together with CSR 2. CSR 2 explained everything to CSR 3 via the chat, and when CSR 3 said, "Okay, I have it from here," CSR 2 left. Like her two predecessors, CSR 3 was very kind and sympathetic to Christine's problem. Things started to progress when—yes, you guessed it—the Internet connection blinked again and the chat session ended.

At this point, Christine decided she really needed to hear someone's voice, not only because of the shaky Internet, but because she feared she had lost all of her files in the attempted transfer and she needed reassurance. With the Internet connection restored, she clicked on an area that listed alternate contact methods and called an 800 number listed. Within a couple of easy prompts, she was talking to CSR 4 who promptly did three things: she told Christine why she was calling using the accumulated call notes, she gave Christine her direct contact information in case there was another disconnect, and then she told her that she was taking full ownership of the issue right through to the end.

Though Christine is a technology neophyte of sorts, CSR 4 worked with her patiently. She never made her feel stupid or

talked over her head. She guided her to a screen-sharing service
and walked her through the attempts to rectify the problem, keeping her in the loop every step of the way. At one point, there was a
sixty-minute process that had to complete, so CSR 4 gave Christine
her direct contact information again and told her to call her back
when it was done. Hesitant to hang up, she did as requested. She
called CSR 4 and left a message when the operation was complete,
worried she may never hear back. Pleasantly surprised again, CSR
4 personally called her back within five minutes then stuck with
her, right through to the final resolution of the problem.

Did you make note of what went well? In relaying this story
to me, Christine had some awesome things to say about her experience that day. She said every one of the people she dealt with
made her feel like they actually cared about her problem despite
her panic. She said they were amazingly polite and patient. She
said that she felt like she was being helped by someone she knew,
like a friend. She said she never felt stupid at any point in the
interaction.

Now, remember—Christine is the one who gets the not-so-fun
job of calling in to support whenever we need it. She said that
she was "stunned" at how good the support was because in her
experience, it is so rare. She actually went to the trouble to tell
CSR 4 just how great she thought the interaction was. Later that
day around the dinner table, she said to me, "What is the secret
ingredient that makes these particular people so good? Do they
get paid more? Do they get trained better? Do they give them
better benefits? Why can't every other company be like this?"
Good question, honey . . . good question.

I saved the best part for last. She closed the conversation with
me by saying something so significant, so imperative to the entire
point of this book, that every one of you should read it carefully
and more than once:

"John, that was far and away the best support I have ever had and I would NEVER own anything but an Apple product again, because every time I have ever had to deal with them, whether by phone or in the store, they are *mind-blowingly awesome*."

You better get to that Extra Scoop. Don't you agree?

<u>Your Chapter 4 Extra Scoop</u>
Remember that reading words from a page is not communication. When there is a lack of good communication, your Customers will assume the worst, and they are probably right.

CHAPTER 5

Whatever Happened to People and Things I Could Understand?

Here is a funny line for you: "Why do you ask me to press one for English when you are going to connect me with someone who can barely speak it?" You're not laughing. I get it, trust me.

Please know that I intend no disrespect to people of other dialects or nationalities. I know many people in both categories and have wonderful colleagues from across the pond, as they say. The cold, hard reality is that it can be nearly impossible to understand certain people—or their names—because of their accent and/or dialect.

There is nothing politically correct about forcing your Customers to feel that they need to be culturally sensitive to people they cannot understand and struggle to communicate with. How many times have your Customers called in, received a greeting that makes no sense to them, and after asking for the person to repeat, they get back the same unintelligible sentences? Folks, don't do this.

Here is the appropriate response to a Customer who does not understand a CSR:

> "Yes, my speech can be a challenge for some. Let me slow it down, but know that if my speech is

still difficult for you to understand, I would be
glad to transfer you to another CSR who you may
be better able to understand. It's no problem at all.
Would you like me to do that for you now?"

I had to call in to a technical support line to get a return mate-
rial authorization (RMA) process started for one of my Customers
(please note my Extra Scoop—I did this for my Customer. I didn't
make them struggle with it). After waiting on hold for at least
twenty minutes, a person finally came on the line. He said his
name (which I could not make out) and several other unintelligible sentences, but I did make out the words "help" and "you."
When the pause occurred post his scripted initial introduction, I
just figured that was my queue to speak. I let him know the problem we were having and that the product was under warranty,
so I would like to get an RMA. I wish I could tell you what was
said next, but the fact is I can't. The person on the other end of the
line might as well have been speaking Klingon (yes, I am a Star
Trek fan). I politely said, "Could you please say that again and
talk a little slower? I am having trouble understanding you." He
did his best to oblige, but the result was just . . . well . . . slower
Klingon. We battled (key word) through a few more sentences
before I finally just asked him to please get someone else on the
phone, which he did. The result? More Klingon. I finally was able
to exchange enough information with this group of people to get
an e-mail explaining the RMA process. I breathed a sigh of relief
knowing I could do the rest by e-mail.

There can be a big difference between knowing English and
knowing the English language. Your people must understand the
nuances of the language, and it is amazing how many companies
struggle with this. Remember that frustration-free notion I mentioned earlier? If Customers cannot understand your people, they

are going to get frustrated very quickly and in some cases, the CSR is wrongly going to get frustrated right back.

A person called in to tech support with an Internet browser problem for a second time. After great difficulty in communicating with the CSR due to accent, she was gruffly told by the CSR that the browser she was using was not supported. She went on to explain she had called in a few weeks earlier and that the CSR she spoke to at that time told her the browser was the one she should use and now did not know what she was to do. After a number of difficult back-and-forth exchanges, the CSR practically shouted, "You are not listening to me. Stop talking and listen." Obviously, the Customer got upset and let that CSR know she would not tolerate being spoken to in that way and that she wanted to speak to a manager, at which time she was promptly hung up on.

In calling back, she got another CSR and again explained the situation. This CSR came clean and let her know that the particular browser she was trying to use was a gray area for them and they did not have a clear direction. He was patient and helped her load a different browser, and on the way she went, but not before filing a complaint with the team's manager about that first CSR. Whose job is it to listen to whom? Whose job is it to understand whom?

One of my favorite comedians is Tim Hawkins. He does a great bit about his own solution for solving a computer problem, and while it might not be perfectly relevant to this topic, you know you have been frustrated enough to do it his way. Check it out by going to YouTube and searching for "Tim Hawkins technical difficulties."

What are you saying to your Customer when you are blatantly putting people on the front lines who are nearly impossible to understand? You are telling them that there are far more important things to you than delivering a great experience to them—

that's what you are saying. By the way, does anyone else see the irony in the fact that no one *ever* complains about not understanding the person on the other end of "Presione dos para español" (Push two for Spanish)? Literally. It seems we can provide plenty of understandable people who can speak Spanish but cannot provide plenty of understandable people who can speak English clearly. Give me a break!

Am I beating up on this point? You're darn right I am. And it is *so* easy to fix this. You have a number of options:

1) If you think it's hard to find English-speaking people, you need to go no farther than your backyard. There are thousands of good people drowning in college debt (don't get me started on the state of higher education) who need good jobs. You might be thinking that they don't want to work in Customer Service and if true, you've only yourselves to blame. It's hard to want to work in departments with the reputation of delivering horrible Customer experiences or only hiring inexpensive offshore labor. Maybe they have experienced poor interactions for themselves. Remember the ambivalence we spoke about in Chapter 2? CSRs get frustrated because they spend their day talking to frustrated Customers whom they can rarely help. Then the Customers get more frustrated, then no one wants to be a CSR.

2) If you are bent on delivering service from offshore (and there are some good reasons to have this, like "Follow the Sun" support), bring in professionals to tutor your employees in proper English and enunciation. They need to understand English from more than just a dictionary perspective.

Make sure that before they even get to the front lines, they pass oral testing delivered by a control group of would-be Customers. Oh, and make sure that testing is delivered by phone.

3) Make sure there is a path to escalate the Customer to a team that speaks great English. Just like you might have an escalation team for specific sets of problems, you can have an escalation team for those who struggle to understand your front-line people. Maybe this team is located onshore.

4) Grade your people for communication capabilities. If they are consistently getting people frustrated or having to escalate to your "English team," it's time to find them a new position or a new company to work for.

5) Offer your Customers multiple ways to communicate, like online chat and e-mail. Now, you are not hearing me tell you to invent ways to not talk to people. It is equally frustrating to not be able to get a human on the phone when you need help. Even with other ways to communicate, one survey noted that nearly half of all Customers prefer to communicate by phone.

You should also note that communication by other methods does not necessarily equal flawless communication, so let's talk about that next.

THE E-MAIL FIASCO

I needed assistance on a software product which I had been providing as a service to my Customers. I sent in a service request by e-mail since that was my only option (problem already). I received an e-mail back—"Thank you for your request"—and a second one shortly thereafter asking for additional information, which I provided. What transpired from there was a swift, downward trek to aggravation. I next received an e-mail saying, "We received your request," even though I wasn't requesting a thing—I was fulfilling their request to me. Hours later, I received another e-mail stating, "We haven't heard from you, please reply."

I e-mailed them again, saying, "Yes, you have heard from me, but I didn't hear from you except for an e-mail from you telling me otherwise."

Next e-mail: "We received your request." Grrrr. Next e-mail from them: "Did you read the notes in the e-mail?"

I replied, "There were no notes in the e-mail," and copy/pasted the e-mail back to them so they could see that. Now, you might be thinking we should be near the end of this, but oh no, my friends, it gets better.

Next e-mail: "Thank you for your request." *Sigh*, whatever. Hours later: "We haven't heard from you." Okie dokie. Now, I have had enough. I could follow the Tim Hawkins methodology and shoot my computer, but instead my next e-mail let them know how poor their support was and that I couldn't resell their services if this is what my Customers would potentially deal with. It was only then that I got a personal e-mail—not an automated e-mail—saying, "I am sorry about this. Please see the notes below." I promise you they were not nearly as sorry as I was, but the notes gave me the answer I needed, sort of. It wasn't the one I wanted, but I got an answer and after that mess, I could live with that.

The only positive thing that transpired in the entire interaction was a suggestion to e-mail the Customer-feedback team to let them know about my experience. Still, I wondered to myself why they couldn't do it themselves. Do they not care enough about the experience they provided to let someone upstairs know something isn't working?

Automated e-mails are dangerous. What do your automated e-mails tell your Customers? You might consider paring them down to the bare essentials, like this: "We have received your request, which is number 12345-9876, and you can expect a reply in 24–48 hours for most issues." E-mail communication has a place, like supplementing your human CSR teams, but please do not provide e-mail support as the only option for a Customer. Form e-mails back from your team are going to do little good when what the Customer really needs is someone to understand their problem.

AUTOMATED AGONY

Automated attendants and interactive voice response (IVR) systems can provide some positive things for your Customers. Done properly, they can provide easy direction to the help they need, set a professional tone, and offer positive self-help and answers to frequently asked questions while in queue for assistance.

By now, you know that I will assert that automated attendants and IVR systems are often deployed with little thought to a Customer's experience. You might find a theme in this book to be to think through what is reasonable for the Customer. Consider:

- How long is it reasonable to make someone wait for help? A recent report found that long hold times were a key Customer Service pain point and further suggested that slashing hold times is an area where 57 percent of those polled believe businesses could improve.[5]

---

[5] Ibid.

- How long is it reasonable to listen to an automated attendant before I can actually know what selection I should make to get to the right person? This is not an exaggeration: on one call for technical support, it literally took me one minute and forty-nine seconds to finally get in to the queue that I needed to for help. That might not sound long on paper, but the next time you have something more important to do, stop and pick up a phone and hold it to your ear for nearly two minutes.

- How reasonable is it to completely shield a Customer support phone number from your patrons? What do you think that communicates to them? Well, it communicates exactly what you think: That you can't be bothered to help me, you are not interested in helping, or that you can't spare the profit margin to properly do so. Maybe it's all of those things. I can tell you this: I no longer will do business with anyone who cannot readily provide me with a phone number to call, and I don't mean that it's okay to hide it on a "Contact Us" page, either! I actually was looking to provide a specific wireless solution to my Customers, only to determine that there was no way whatsoever to call the manufacturer. Next!

- Is it reasonable for you to ask me a dozen questions after I have waited on hold forever, even though your IVR system *easily* identified who I was and what I was calling about? True story:

    I dial in to a Customer Service number.
    IVR: Is this John Mamon calling from 555-1234?
    Press 1 for yes, 2 for no. (I press 1.)
    IVR: If you have an existing case number, enter it now, otherwise press 2 for additional options. (I enter my case number.)

IVR: I see you are calling about your problem with "xyz widget." Do you still need help with this? Press 1 for yes or 2 for additional options. (I press 1)

IVR: Got it. Please stay on the line and someone will be with you momentarily.

Ten minutes go by and a CSR finally comes on the line.

CSR: May I have your name please?

ME: Well, sure. It's John Mamon, but don't you know that already?

CSR: No, sir. Is this an existing case or are you opening a new one?

ME: It's an existing one, but don't you know that already?

CSR: No. What is your case number?

ME: I punched the case number in to the phone system and that's how I got routed to you.

CSR: Sir, I have no access to that information.

Point made. The absurdity that an IVR knows more than your CSRs . . .

- Is it reasonable to try to sell me more products and services via automated messaging before I have even gotten someone to help me with my problem? I actually called in to a support number and the automated attendant could not stop telling me about all the great products and services I could buy *before* I was even presented with my "Press 1 for . . ." options.
  - * Let me help you with this one—it is not reasonable at all. Trust me, I get the upsell. But in order to sell me what you want me to buy, you

must first provide me the Customer Service I believe I deserve. Remember, I am probably already frustrated because I have to call you for help on something I already own. I am in no frame of mind to listen to your sales pitch at this point. Let's try this *after* you deliver me a great Customer Service experience. You could say, "I see you may be eligible for an upgrade. Would you like me to connect you with a representative who can help you with that?" You could send me an e-mail telling me about other products or services you have, including a discount for any inconvenience. You could offer me new services and special savings for filling out a Customer Service survey. Right after you've provided me great Customer Service and I am feeling good about myself for doing business with your company—that's the time to reel me in.

- Is it reasonable to trap a Customer in an IVR system with no way to get to a human being?
    * Let me say this: the companies who get Customer support right will be the victors in the end, and—borrowing from a previous chapter—providing a great entrance from an IVR perspective is a great start. Check out a recent commercial from Discover (Go to YouTube and search for "Live Customer Service Discover It card commercial." There is more than one in the series). Make particular note of the fact that Discover is claiming you can talk to a person in the *United States* day or night. How refreshing . . .

ALWAYS KNOW WHAT YOU ARE TELLING YOUR CUSTOMER

Another common theme you have likely picked up on is to always be aware of what you are saying to your Customer without actually saying anything.

- Are you communicating to me that I am important to you and you want me to be your Customer forever, or are you communicating that you are glad I bought your product and you hope and pray I never contact you again?
- Are you indicating there is something more important than my complete satisfaction?
- Are you communicating that you absolutely do not want me to call you and that I am on my own?
- Are you suggesting that you would rather have your fingers pounded flat one by one with a hammer rather than help me?

I was standing in line at a service establishment. There were nine of us in line. There were six people behind the counter. There was only one person of the six actually servicing the line. A couple stared blankly at their computers. A couple more were talking about where they were going to lunch. Hey people, *wake up*! Worst of all, I was in line more than thirty minutes only to find out I was not in the line I was supposed to be in. Surely someone could have jumped in and helped. Surely someone could have come from behind the counter to see if there was anyone they could help (like me). What do you suppose all those people in line were thinking as they witnessed this? As if I have to tell you . . .

53

I was at a paid event and approached the check-in table. Two people working the table were talking about their weekend. I stood there for about thirty seconds before I politely said, "Excuse me?" Neither of them skipped a beat in their conversation. They didn't even look at me. Finally, I reached over the counter and irritably grabbed the stack of preprinted name tags which was right next to a cash box. That sure got their attention . . .

A person had gone in to a coffee shop and placed an order. The person who made the drink handed it to the Customer with her back to her while she carried on a conversation about her boyfriend. The drink was made wrong, and the worker made the person feel rude just because she had to finally interrupt the conversation forcefully in order to let her know about the error.

Whether you want to acknowledge it or not, everything you do communicates something to your Customer. What do you want to say? Is it so hard to acknowledge your Customer? Is it so hard to get your CSRs to work seamlessly with your systems? Is it that difficult to communicate effectively to your English-speaking Customers? You are creating an experience one way or the other and that experience is measurable—ranging from awful to awesome. So which one will you provide?

Adding an Extra Scoop is critical. Don't you agree?

Your Chapter 5 Extra Scoop
It is your CSRs' responsibility to understand the Customer, not the Customers' responsibility to understand your CSR.

CHAPTER 6

Whatever Happened to the Customer Is Always Right?

I don't know who first coined it, but there is an old adage:

> Rule #1: The Customer is always right.
> Rule #2: When the Customer is wrong, refer to Rule #1.

Many of us are taught from the get-go in business that the Customer is always right. It's a clever line. I wonder if the real meaning has become misconstrued over the years. It should not mean that the Customer has the right to be belligerent and irrational, nor does it mean that the Customer should be able to make any demand whatsoever to which the company is obligated to comply. Here's what I think it means:

> There is almost no reasonable issue presented by
> a Customer that should not be generally satisfied
> by a provider.

There's that word *reasonable* again, and it's important that the people on the front lines are capable of making a determination on what is in fact reasonable. Don't get too hung up on that side of the discussion, though. Spend more time focusing on how you can satisfy each need.

On the flip side, we know that not all Customers are reasonable, which in turn means the Customer is *not* always right. This, however, is a small minority of your Customers (if it isn't, you have a much, much bigger problem). You should interact with unreasonable Customers as best as you can, but there are limits on accommodating them. After all, some of your Customers are just going to be plain crazy. And if you don't realize that, you haven't spent enough time at the Customer Service counter or on your Customer Service phone lines.

While the Customer is not always right, it is important to realize that how they *feel* typically is right. Very often Customers make mistakes or don't understand the service or accidentally break the product right after purchase. Still, they are going to call in hoping that you can help them in some way. After all, if you can't help them, what is their alternative? Customers calling in for help can feel:

- Frustrated because they have to take time to call
- Irritated that the product or service is not functioning as it should
- Embarrassed that they know they created the problem themselves
- Helpless because you may hold the only key to the solution
- Fear that the problem cannot be solved
- Anxiety due to some external pressure to get it resolved

These are already pretty negative emotions to deal with. Now pile on feeling:

- Exasperation because they have been talking with multiple people for an hour and are no closer to a solution
- Anger because they cannot understand the CSRs or communicate with anyone

- Upset due to a long hold time
- Defeated because they cannot get a resolution

It is easy to see how difficult it can be not only for a Customer, but for a CSR to overcome these feelings. You must acknowledge these emotions exist and that they are valid. You can argue a fact, but you can't argue with how someone feels. Your CSRs need to know this truth even better than you. There is nothing more important than how your Customer feels when the service transaction is over (like when they hang up the phone). Know that how they feel when they hang up the phone after speaking to one of your CSRs largely determines whether or not they will be a repeat Customer for your business or tell other potential Customers positive things about you.

"Mr. Customer, here is what I *can* do for you . . ."

So, now we accept that the Customer's feelings are always right, but there are circumstances when the Customer's request for help is either unreasonable or the solution is out of reach. When all else fails, there is such a thing as compromise.

A compromising posture by your CSRs sets a tone for the conversation that turns it from negative (I have a problem and I am unhappy) to positive (here is a solution and you can now feel relieved). The Customer feels heard, and this alone can ease negative feelings. "That seems to be a unique problem that we haven't experienced before, and I am sorry that has been your experience. Here is what I am going to do to make things right for you . . ." The Customer does not feel wrong or senseless; instead, they feel valued. The CSR feels empowered to help. The company retains a Customer and may gain referrals from the experience. Everybody wins.

Here is a supporting story. As mentioned prior, I have had my insurance with the same carrier for a very long time by any standard—nearly twenty years. At some point in the not-too-distant past, the carrier decided that they were going with paperless billing. By itself, this is typically no big deal, as you can opt out of such "services," except that my carrier decided to tie my discount to the use of their e-bill system. Now, you have probably picked up on the fact I am a bit "old school." I have been paying my bills using the exact same methodology for many years and that process requires the receipt of a paper bill. When I tried to opt out, the CSR thought it was of no issue, but what he didn't know is that I would in fact lose a discount according to the online system. My solution seemed out of reach, but here is what he did:

"Mr. Mamon, I totally understand that you want a paper bill and I know you have been with us a long time. I can't override the system and get you out of the e-bill program without affecting your discount. But, here is what I *can* do for you. I am setting a reminder every month in our system for our team to print and send you a bill ourselves. I will personally see to it."

That was a terrific compromise and one I found would reasonably solve my issue. I felt good about that, the CSR solved a problem for a longtime Customer, and I am still very much a happy Customer today. See? Everybody wins.

Whether you take responsibility for everything under the sun that your Customer might demand (some can and do—see Walmart) is really an inconsequential point. Regardless of whether the point is fair to the company, the Customer is still worth making happy: they still are likely to buy again if you *make it right*; they still will tell others good things if you take care of them. So, instead of fighting them on what is at the end of the day an inconsequential point, choose to be accommodating and help them out. The idea that the company will somehow be irreparably harmed because Customers will line up in droves to take advantage of your accommodating nature is, well, kind of foolish. Oh, and if you are thinking, "Jeez, John, if you only knew my people, they'd give away the farm if we did that," just stop it. Every smart company has a "Returns and Allowances" bucket in their financials and you can easily build boundaries for what CSRs can do with and without escalation and additional approvals.

As a quick side point to this, companies cannot allow themselves to fall into a "transactional profit" trap. You cannot look at the Customer and say, "We only made seven dollars on that transaction. Shipping them a new part would exceed our profit and we would lose money on that Customer." The sum value of a satisfied Customer exceeds the value of the transaction's profit. That's a good one—you should highlight that!

Satisfied Customer > The related transaction's profit

AMAZON GIVES AN EXTRA SCOOP

I bought something from Amazon recently and when it arrived, it wasn't the correct item. It was disappointing for my daughter, but I thought, "Hey, things happen and it's Amazon, so I'll just call and get it replaced." So I called up Amazon and it turns out what I purchased was bought *through* Amazon but not *from* Amazon, so Amazon was not responsible for the product and therefore did not guarantee it.

You see where this is going, but wait. There's a really great story here and it didn't take five angry phone calls to make it happen. In fact, I didn't even suggest to the CSR what she was about to do.

She took me very carefully and politely through how Amazon and the relationships between external vendors worked. As she spoke, I sat with my head in my hand figuring that the end of this story was going to be that I was plain out of luck. Near the end of the explanation the CSR said, "You know what, Mr. Mamon? I am really sorry this happened to you, and I see you are a good Customer, so I am going to go ahead and give you a full refund anyway. Plus, I am going to get another one shipped to you right away from another vendor."

My head rose suddenly and I had to shake it vigorously, thinking I may have dozed off and started dreaming. Per the epiphany I have shared with you, I have been conditioned to expect a less-than-good experience, so there was no way this could be real. In fact, it was real. She said, "Will that be okay for you?"

"Of course," I replied. "Thank you so much for handling this the way you have. You exceeded my expectations." I could hear her smile through the phone.

It is awfully hard for an online retailer to create a sense of personal touch, so it's even more critical to provide great Customer Service. If nothing else, I find Amazon to be a great, Customer-oriented company. Was this hard for the CSR at Amazon to do? I don't think so. I think she was smart, caring, and trained that not only did it make sense to take care of a Customer's problem, but sometimes it makes sense to go well above and beyond what someone might consider normal. The result of this interaction? I am going to buy the very first thing Amazon sells by helicopter drone. Okay maybe not, but you can bet I shop a lot on Amazon and do so more freely with the knowledge that they will always take care of me. Amazon has a loyal and happy Customer who will go out of his way to find more things to buy from Amazon. I will probably even tell others what a great experience I have with them. Hey, I just did!

A TALE OF TWO CAR COMPANIES

A young woman had the misfortune of sliding on the ice and hitting a curb sideways in her brand-new car, which caused damage to the steering. If only her misfortune had stopped there. She took it to the dealership where she bought the car to have it repaired. When she picked the car up, she realized it strongly pulled to the right. She called them back and told them the problem and they had her bring it back. She picked it up when they told her it was ready, except that it still wasn't fixed. This bring-it-back, fix-it, return-it-again carousel continued a few more times until she demanded to speak to the manager. The service department apparently didn't see a problem with the steering, so they never actually fixed it.

When she met the manager, he acted friendly and suggested they go for a drive to see what the problem was. She demonstrated the drift to the right. Clearly irritated, he suggested they switch places so he could drive. As he drove, he took his hands off the wheel and showed the car did not drift to the right—except she noticed that his left thumb was discreetly holding the steering wheel to prevent the drift. When she called him out on it, he became more irritated but reluctantly said he would call the insurance company for her and get new parts ordered.

From that point forward, the dealership treated her like she was the irritant. Though hard to believe, she actually picked up her car three more times and the problem still had not been solved. Even worse, they stopped calling to tell her the car was ready. She had to call and essentially harass them. When she took her car in for the final time, the service manager told her in a scolding tone, "You can have a loaner car for three days."

She said, "What if you haven't fixed my car in that time?"

In an even more stern voice, he said, "You have three days!" The message he was sending was clear to her: She was wrong, she was an annoyance, and she was taking advantage of them.

She was humiliated and furious. She vowed to never buy that brand again. And thirty-plus years later, she never has. Not only that, but she passed this story on to her four children, and they have never bought that brand either to this day.

In contrast, the Saturn Car Company came into being several years later. This company, an offspring of GM, was set up to build quality, comfortable, attractive cars at an affordable price. Their tag line was "A different kind of car company," and they did their very best to live up to that slogan in every way. When Saturn announced its first recall in February 1991, dealer technicians drove to where the owners were just to replace a seat bracket on about 1,200 cars. A few months later, Saturn learned a supplier had provided a batch of improperly formulated antifreeze that might cause engine damage. Instead of replacing the antifreeze, Saturn replaced more than 1,100 cars. That's right—in both cases, they didn't tell the Customer to bring it in so they could make a repair at the Customer's (in)convenience. Instead, they proactively got their ice-cream scoop out and piled it on.

Which company hurt its brand? Which company likely didn't retain a loyal Customer(s) when it was over? In spite of tens of thousands of dollars in more short-term expenses, which company got great referrals, great publicity, and as a result, a lot more sales? Which company clearly had the mindset of "the Customer is always right"?

Adding an Extra Scoop is the right thing to do. Wouldn't you agree?

Your Chapter 6 Extra Scoop
How the Customer feels when the transaction is over is the
***only* thing that matters—nothing else.**

CHAPTER 7

*Whatever Happened to Saying What You Do and
Doing What You Say?*

So much of providing a good Customer experience is establishing mutually reasonable expectations—that is saying what you do—and then meeting, or better yet, exceeding those expectations—that's doing what you say. Please know that I recognize that the sentiments around saying what you do and doing what you say reach further into people and companies that just Customer Service (or at least they should), but we will stick with that facet here. It's time for a formula:

> Mutually reasonable expectations + saying
> what you do + doing what you say = A positive
> environment for a Customer experience

First, a word about mutually reasonable expectations. It's critically important that expectations are in fact mutually reasonable. To be clear, it is not mutually reasonable for a Customer to expect instantaneous resolution when the industry standard is thirty minutes. It's not mutually reasonable for them to expect one-hour delivery when the standard is two business days. Likewise, it is not reasonable for you to set an expectation of two hours/five business days (respectively). When it comes to mutually reasonable expectations, common sense and reasonableness are at least half the equation, and Customer need and demand drives the rest. Now, there is nothing wrong with a company's value proposition or its unique selling point to be to provide faster service. That's okay, and I am not talking about that. I am saying that the expectations with your Customers should be fair and reasonable.

Saying what you do is communicating to the Customer what they can and should expect from you. It is said that nature abhors a vacuum, and so do Customers. If you don't set their expectations, they will make their own, and then you are set up to fail. Part of setting expectations is posting/providing/communicating information. Here is an example from a web page:

> Prefer to call us? Our number is 555-123-4567. Please expect a two- to four-minute wait for assistance. We can more quickly help you if you have your serial number ready.

Another important thing to do in setting expectations is to acknowledge your challenges—let people know. For example, let's say you are experiencing a problem with a specific part or service. Do you put that in bold letters on the home page of your website? Do you have it as part of your phone system's up-front messages? Or, do you let Customer after Customer call in and wait forever in a queue, just to tell them about the problem with the part or service and that there is nothing you can do right now?

Owning up to a failure or a shortcoming is one of the best ways for your company to create a good Customer experience. In reality, unless you are a surgeon, everyone understands when someone makes an honest mistake or has a service challenge, so long as they work to correct it. Customers *love* authenticity.

Having tackled saying what we do, you should know this: nothing will wreck a Customer experience more than committing to something and then failing to do it. I am absolutely astounded at how I run into people and companies not doing what they say on a daily basis. I hear everything from "I will call you tomorrow" to "we will arrive onsite by two o'clock p.m." and then, almost expectantly, they fail to do so. The Customer has expectations and you helped to set them, so meet them. We all know people who were promised furniture delivery at 10:00 a.m. but got it at 6:00 p.m., the daily progress and status never reaching them. We all know people who had a utility scheduled for 1:00 p.m., and at 5:00 p.m. they got a call saying the crew was not doing any more work that day and they would have to come tomorrow. (By the way, who pays for the vacation day you had to use to be there?)

Doing what you say demonstrates your commitment to the Customer and their experience. Doing what you say means you can be trusted; that you can be counted upon to deliver. That's the kind of reputation your company needs and certainly should want. Doing what you say (or not) has a massive impact on your brand image. Inconsistency in this area will typically have a major impact on Customer retention.

A company that purchased a voice-over-IP (VoIP) phone service relayed this story to me. They purchased the service because they were told it was the exact same service as if they bought the premise-based version. As it turns out, it wasn't (say what you do: grade F). The representative said they would fix it, but they didn't (do what you say: grade F). The company made several attempts to escalate the issue before they finally gave up and asked for outside help. The resolution in the end? They found a new provider.

That's a lost Customer and the consultant that ended up helping them isn't very likely to recommend them in the future.

FAILURE TO COMMUNICATE

So, I have established mutually reasonable expectations, say what I do and do what I say. I am all set, right? Not always. Sometimes, you simply fail to deliver. Stuff happens. If you are in business long enough, a bunch of "stuffs" will happen. Key point: it's not about the failure; it's about how you handle the failure. It is absolutely vital to communicate during such a time. Another recurring theme in this book that is not hard to do. Let's explore further.

When you fail to meet expectations and/or commitments, follow this "Missed Commitment" recipe:

1) Own up to the failure, apologize, and express sympathy (acknowledge/apologize/sympathize).
2) Explain what has transpired.
3) Reset the Customer's expectations.
4) Offer something for the inconvenience. This can be a small token like a free upgrade or a coupon for future use, or it can be something you could incorporate into your brand promise ("If we don't complete your work on time, it's free").

Let's look at some examples of failures.

Problem: I will call you back tomorrow (and never do).

This is a failure to do what you say. Be sure you have a good CRM and that you have sound policies for its use. Track unreturned calls/missed appointments by your CSRs. Each CSR should have an ID number and a direct extensions/call-back number that is given out to your Customers without asking. For instance: "Hello, my name is Grace. My CS ID number is 12345 . . ." Are your CSRs, or perhaps some of your CSRs, hiding behind anonymity? The acid test is if your Customer cannot call back in and speak to the CSR they spoke to yesterday; if they cannot, then they are.

I had a problem with a communications company and called in about it. The CSR assured me that a service manager would call me back within twenty-four hours. I would say I am still waiting, but instead I changed services to another company at around the five-week mark.

Problem: Your service will be complete on *x* day and time.
Remember my trailer story?

Problem: We will be there between 9:00 a.m. and 2:00 p.m.
Seriously? You do realize that people have lives, right? This is not a mutually reasonable expectation. Most families have two working parents. Do you actually expect them to take a half day of vacation so you can show up whenever you are good and ready? This is an unreasonable burden to place upon your Customers. I categorically state that this practice is unacceptable. There are entirely too many systems, processes, and people available to provide a much more accurate expectation for your Customer; you simply haven't bothered to spend the time and money to figure it out. There are multiple paths to a solution based on your business model and discussing each of them is beyond the scope of this book, but I will share one perspective.

I had the good fortune of meeting the COO of a local pest-control company that is rapidly expanding. I was meeting him to discuss something entirely different, but we quickly realized we had a common passion for Customer Service. Unprompted, he told me that one of their keys to success is making sure they set specific expectations for appointments and meet them every time.

They do not give arrival time ranges because "[they] know that someone is at home when they probably should be at their job. [They] know that [they] can't impose on someone's day to the extent that they can't pick up their kids from school or make other appointments." This pest-control company gives specific appointment times and they have people dedicated to ensuring a service person is onsite for the appointment fifteen minutes *before* the set arrival time. If that person is not fifteen minutes early, they are late. If something happens and they are not going to make it on time, they roll another truck. Now that, my friends, is saying what you do and doing what you say.

Problem: We will be there between 9:00 a.m. and 2:00 p.m. (and no one shows).

So, on top of an unreasonable time window, you don't even show up? This is a failure to do what you say. Things happen and we can all understand that. When your representative will not be there in the specified time frame, you need to call well in advance. Don't have your service person call at 4:00 p.m. or 4:30 and say they are running late. Your service person knew at least two hours beforehand they were running late. Telling me after the fact is only going to get your ear chewed off. See the "Missed Commitment" recipe above.

Problem: Order placed, shipping information sent, but product never arrives.

Another failure to *do what you say*, and this story is personal. I placed an order for some equipment with two-day expedited shipping because we needed it in a hurry. The CSR took all my information and set my expectations as to when I should receive it. I even received both order and shipping confirmations by e-mail, but two days later, no equipment. I called in the next morning, gave them my order number, and was abruptly told that the order was cancelled. "Who cancelled it?" I asked disbelievingly.

"We cancelled the order."

I waited for an explanation but with none forthcoming, I asked why.

"We could not ship to the address you gave us."

"So that's it?" I replied. "No phone call? No notification? You just cancelled it? The CSR I spoke to when I placed the order assured me I would have it in my hands yesterday. I paid for two-day shipping and I need that equipment. Now what am I supposed to do (besides find another provider for future orders)?"

"I am sorry," he said. "We can place the order again with a different address." Gee, thanks.

Problem: Advertised special not available.

This is an example of "stuff happens." Upon one man's arrival at a merchant, the special he came in for was not available as advertised. A representative did her best to handle it, but could not explain why it had happened, nor did she offer anything to compensate him for the inconvenience. How could this have gone better? Glad you asked:

"Sir, I am very sorry for the inconvenience. I know it is a disappointment to you and it is one for us, too (Step 1—acknowledge/apologize/sympathize). Headquarters messed up the advertisement and by the time we found out, it was too late to fix it (Step 2—explain what has transpired). We are supposed to have the advertised items in the store within three days (Step 3—reset expectations). We pride ourselves in doing a good job and we value our Customers, so we are offering the same deal on the upgraded model we do have in the store, so you will get a better unit for the same special price (Step 4—offer something for the inconvenience)."

This kind of communication makes your Customer feel great. It makes them feel respected and important to the company. Let's finish with two more stories that serve as a contrast in doing what you say.

A man I know told me about a time he needed to take his car in for repairs. The dealer had a team look over the car and came back with an estimate for the work. He signed off on the work and went about his day. When he went in to pick up his car the next day, the bill was nearly 20 percent less than the estimate—quite a nice surprise. The service representative explained that the repairs took less time than expected so the charges were not quite as high as they originally thought. The service rep also told him that while they were doing the work, they topped off all of his fluids and washed the car for him as a complimentary service. How about that—exceeding expectations and an Extra Scoop to boot! No wonder he told me he takes his car to the same shop every time.

Different person and a different experience: a woman took her vehicle in for brake service. She received a quote and authorized the service. She received a call letting her know the vehicle was ready. When she went to pick up the car, the bill was 20 percent higher. Alarmed, she demanded to know why the bill exceeded the estimate. The service manager explained that they had missed a part that they needed. It was only after a bitter discussion between the service manager and the woman's husband that the service manager decided to discount the repairs. How about that—poorly set expectations and a reluctance to make it right. That's not an Extra Scoop; that's a scoop on the floor.

As a sidenote to this story, you should take special care to avoid sexism in your Customer Service ranks. I am afraid that treating women differently, like talking down to them and treating them as though they couldn't possibly know what you are talking about, does still exist out there, particularly in certain industries. CSRs should not assume that because the Customer is female, she is less informed, less capable, or less deserving of respect. It is unfortunate that the husband needed to get involved in the above story.

FLYING THE (NOT SO) FRIENDLY SKIES

The airline industry is fairly well known for regularly failing to do what they say, mostly around departure and arrival times. Since most of us have experienced this at one point or another, we are going to use them as an example and then see how we can learn from them to improve your company's Customer Service experience.

Some of the problems the airlines have are beyond their control. Things like weather, congestion, and mechanical problems can have horrendous results on a Customer's experience. Mechanical problems create delays; thunderstorms can wreak havoc on flight paths. This of course is all reasonable because it is generally out of the control of the airline. After all, would we really want to fly in a plane with mechanical problems in the name of staying on schedule? Here's the rub. It is very difficult for us as the Customer to distinguish between what delays and inconveniences the airlines can and cannot control because they communicate these things so poorly.

Key point: In the absence of truth, people make up their own, and that fabricated truth is rarely in your favor as the service provider. Without proper communication, your Customers will conclude that you are poor at Customer Service, lying to them, taking advantage of them, hiding something, or maybe all of the above.

In the event of a delay, wouldn't it be great if the gate agents simply walked us through what was going on and helped reset our expectations? To be sure, most people will be frustrated, but at least they can understand what is transpiring and come to terms with the new expectations you have now set. It is certainly better than allowing them to stew in their anger that the plane is now delayed for forty-five minutes and it has to be because your airline is a lousy service company and couldn't keep a time commitment if your collective lives depended upon it.

The airlines got so bad at this, Congress got involved.

"Airline passengers have rights, and these new rules will require airlines to live up to their obligation to treat their Customers fairly," Department of Transportation Secretary LaHood said.[6]

The government of the most powerful nation on the planet had to make rules to be sure airlines treat their Customers fairly. What will it take for you to do it?

Adding an Extra Scoop is the right thing to do. Wouldn't you agree?

Your Chapter 7 Extra Scoop
If you say what you do and do what you say, a significant percentage of your Customers' problems will never even happen.

---

[6] New DOT Consumer Rule Limits Airline Tarmac Delays, Provides Other Passenger Protections." Department of Transportation. December 21, 2009.

CHAPTER 8
Whatever Happened to Taking Ownership?

"Hold My Hand"
—Hootie and the Blowfish

I wouldn't have thought a Hootie and the Blowfish song would have made a good principle for Customer Service (I bet Hootie didn't either), but here it goes.

I was in a particular store location speaking to someone at the register about a few questions that I had. It was a very slow period and thus another service employee was standing and leaning against the counter, thumbing through a magazine. Another Customer walked into the store. The person I was speaking with looked up from our discussion and greeted the Customer warmly. The other representative didn't even bother to look up from his magazine and said nothing. As we returned to our conversation, I noted that the Customer looked a little lost and he quickly thereafter validated that by asking, "Where can I find the motor oil?"

Startled from his disregard, the other service rep responded, "It's on aisle ten, back to the left," as he pointed in the general direction. Just a few moments passed, and the service rep who was speaking with me began to look a bit flustered. He politely asked, "Would you excuse me for just one minute?" As I was in no particular hurry, I obliged. The rep bolted from behind the counter and broke into a trot after the other Customer, saying, "Sir, is it motor oil you are looking for? Let me take you right to it." And so he did.

Two CSRs. Two very different responses to a Customer. One was indifferent; the other was coming unglued at the thought of the Customer being left to fend for himself. One acted like an employee who couldn't wait to go home; the other took the Customer by the hand and took pride in helping him—he acted like the business owner. He held his hand and loved him (in the sense of a company taking care of its Customers) as best as he could. Thanks, Hootie!

Customer satisfaction is an attitude and as I have said, it needs to be intentional. Mercedes-Benz USA wasn't always great at Customer Service. In fact, they were downright poor at it by many accounts. They rested on the laurels of superior engineering and product. That is, until Stephen Cannon came along and made it the number-one priority for the company. He wanted Mercedes to be known for a great Customer experience and launched a full offensive to make it happen. In an interview posted via a blog by Harley Manning, Cannon was asked why he had changed the Customer experience approach. He replied that Customer care has to span every operational area of the company and that a process alone cannot make a Customer smile. He went on to say that you have to "re-architect your organization because the exceptional Customer experience requires equally exceptional people, culture, and leadership."[7] A program called LEAD was created under his watch (Listen, Empathize, Add Value, Delight). His vision and program provided a complete shift in the service they

---

[7] Manning, Harley. "Customer Experience Q&A with Stephen Cannon, President and CEO, Mercedes-Benz USA." Harley Manning's Blog. June 18, 2014.

delivered and what the brand was known for. There was even an entire book written: *Driven to Delight: Delivering World-Class Customer Experience the Mercedes-Benz Way.* My friends, that is intentional.

A trainer walked into a local Mercedes dealer recently to lead a class. There had been little shared with him as to who his contact was and where to go, as he was brought in by a third party. As he walked into the showroom, he spotted two employees. He approached and introduced himself, told them why he was there, and asked if they knew where he should go.

Person A smiled and said she thought it would be the conference room upstairs. She told him she would be glad to help him and made a call to find out for certain where he was to go. She confirmed the location and communicated it to him. Person B looked him in the eye, introduced himself, and welcomed him as he shook his hand. Person B said, "Let me take you there." He offered to help the trainer carry his boxes and guided him up the stairs and through a labyrinth of hallways. As they arrived at the conference room, Person B stayed with him until the trainer's contact showed up, and then politely excused himself. Person B was sharply dressed with a company polo shirt on, and the trainer decided he must be the owner.

Person B, it turns out, was not the owner. He was one of the top salesmen, but you would never know from his behavior that he was not the owner. In the training room, there was a poster from Mercedes-Benz corporate that had keys to treating Customers. Among those keys were:

Know my Customer's name.
Maintain eye contact. Smile. Listen.
Make my Customer feel special.
Value my Customer's time.

At the bottom of the poster was this: "Create a great memory for someone today!"

Taking time out to help a stranger feel so completely comfortable and welcomed may have cost Person B a sale, as his job was to be on the floor helping prospective buyers, not walking some trainer around the building. But that didn't matter. Person B clearly acted like everyone should be treated like a valued Customer. He took this stranger by the hand and took great care of him.

Here's the best part: The trainer told me that he never really thought about buying a Mercedes-Benz, but after his interaction with the people there over the course of that day, the way he felt just being in their presence, he's now looking for a reason to buy a car from them. How great would that be? People who just bump into your company could have such a great experience that they are compelled to do business with you! Write that down.

Could you imagine an owner ignoring someone at the front desk? Could you imagine an owner telling someone to cancel their service and come back in sixty days to get a better price (that is a *true* story)? Really—incent someone to leave your company and sign up with someone else. No way, or they wouldn't be an owner for much longer. Yet these things happen every day.

I know a man named Leo who owns a nice Mexican restaurant. Leo is amazing. He can be seen at any moment doing whatever is necessary to ensure his Customers are happy, whether that is cleaning tables, seating guests—whatever. Moreover, Leo hires people who behave nearly the same way as he does, and I have heard that he has little tolerance for those who don't. I met Leo over fifteen years ago when he ran another restaurant location. No matter how busy he was, Leo always greeted everyone with a huge smile. You can bet I took those good tidings personally. I enjoyed my experience so much I started taking my family there every Friday without exception, even if they weren't in the mood for Mexican cuisine. All along, I just assumed Leo was the owner because of how he acted and the great care he took of everyone and everything around him. I didn't find out until many years later he was "just" the manager. When Leo left the location, it went downhill quickly and when he opened his own place, I became a regular Customer there instead. I love the experience I have when I visit his restaurant. We always shake hands and give each other a "man hug." He comes to our table and spends time with us. He knows my family by name. My wife and daughters obviously know Leo too—the girls were just two and four years old when we first started dining with him. We don't eat Mexican anywhere else, just because of our relationship with Leo.

It doesn't matter what industry you are in; you and each member of your team would do well to behave like Leo. Here is a key point: remember that in any service interaction, you have the potential to create a positive memory or a negative one. Strive to make great memories.

WHY DON'T MORE EMPLOYEES ACT LIKE OWNERS?

I'll provide my answer to this by discussing four contributing factors. Some or all of these might be impacting the quality of Customer Service you are delivering:

1) The training that CSRs receive (if any) often centers around reading from a script and getting off the phone as fast as possible. Even the "Is there anything else I can do for you today?" at the end rings hollow because it is read from a script.

2) CSRs are not empowered to take care of the Customer. They are generally given strict guidelines to follow and very often their only course of action

is to "put you on a brief hold" while they talk to a manager hiding in the background.

3) Culture. CSRs are not screened and hired for the appropriate traits needed to properly *serve* people.

4) There is no direct link between a CSR providing a Customer with an Extra Scoop experience and the benefit they receive for doing so.

We have talked a lot about scripts in a previous chapter, so we won't spend any time on the first factor. Let's discuss the other three factors in more detail.

Factor 2—CSRs are not empowered to take care of the Customer.

I was told a story by a woman who called in to technical support for assistance. After a long, confrontational discussion where she was getting absolutely no satisfaction, she asked to speak to a manager. The CSR said, "No, we don't allow Customers to speak to managers."

Okay, raise your hand if this has happened to you before. It has certainly happened to me. I have asked to speak to a supervisor or manager only to be told that's not possible. In the spirit of our theme, whatever happened to getting to someone who can actually help me? Folks, you have to empower your CSRs to take care of the Customer. Each Customer Service transaction should not be a contest to see who can get off the phone fastest or who can resolve the most cases without giving the Customer anything. Transactions should be measured in the number of smiling, satisfied Customers—period.

Give your CSRs wide boundaries in helping Customers. You can still have approval processes in place to be sure things are being handled appropriately, but really, how much is too much to satisfy a Customer? Would giving a full refund to a Customer in order to save them as a future buyer or a future reference to other buyers be too much? Maybe in your business you think it is, but even still, you can give CSRs a good bit of latitude.

Let me ask you this: if the owner of the company picked up the phone to talk to a Customer in such a scenario, what do you think he or she would do? They would make the problem *go away*. Whatever the Customer's problem was, they would take care of it. They would say, "What would make you happy?" And then they would do it. The owner would never tell the Customer they cannot help. So if the owner would behave that way, why wouldn't you empower others to do the same? Aren't your Customers and your brand important enough? By the way, if the owner wouldn't behave in this way, you have your answer as to why you have poor Customer Service. It starts at the top.

A related sidenote—you need to unequivocally make sure that you are making managers accessible. Sometimes, Customers just need to talk to people who actually have very good interpersonal skills. Sometimes, because you have neglected to empower your CSRs, they want to talk to someone they perceive as having the authority to make them happy. Managers should be accessible even if you enable CSRs to handle any issue. There will always be Customers that will not be satisfied until they talk to someone in authority, and they should be able to. In fact, you want them to because you want your authority figures to hear what's not being fixed by the front line (process or some other failure), who is not doing a good job (training issue), and to protect your employees from hostile people (morale). No matter the case, when someone asks to speak to a manager or supervisor, you need to say, "No problem, let me get them on the phone." I have nothing to add to this statement. It's utterly ridiculous to do anything to the contrary.

Factor 3—Culture. CSRs are not screened and hired for the appropriate traits needed to properly *serve* people.

Not everyone is well suited to be a CSR. Some people just aren't cut out for it. The earlier story of the two service representatives and how they offered help to a Customer demonstrates this fact. Yet companies hire people and put them on the front lines when it's the last place they really want to or should be. It is so important to have the right people in those roles, folks. They may provide the clearest indication to your Customers of the kind of company you are. Sometimes, it may even be their first impression.

I was at lunch with the COO of a growing company and we were talking about Customer Service. He mentioned to me that he had previously worked for Steve Bisciotti, a successful businessman and owner of the Baltimore Ravens. He said that Bisciotti often preached of having a servant mentality when it came to Customer Service. Having a servant mentality is something that doesn't come naturally to everyone, and it is critical to find those kinds of people for your CSR roles. These kinds of people innately want to make people happy. They want to take care of their problems and meet their needs. You may find them actually seeking out people to help in their everyday life.

Southwest Airlines has this mindset in abundance. They believe they can train people to move baggage or clean planes, but if you aren't a happy person, no amount of training will make you one. They have a motto: "Hire for attitude, train for skill." One of Southwest's famous metrics is turnaround time at the gate, and Herb Kelleher directly attributes the success the organization has in this area to hiring people with the right attitude. "Someone who is outgoing and altruistic and can work convivially will be a huge asset," he said. Kelleher also once said, "We tell our people,

'Don't worry about profit. Think about Customer Service.' Profit is a by-product of Customer Service. It's not an end in and of itself."[8] There you have it.

Once you have the right people in the roles, it's important you work to keep them happy. Even people with a servant mentality need to be uplifted and supported. If your CSRs are happy, they will work to make your Customers happy, too. To that end, you need to be on the lookout for people who are not happy in their CSR roles. I live near two different grocery-store chains. Really, they couldn't be more different. In one, you can see that people are just miserable by and large. You feel like an interruption when you ask someone for help. No one is smiling. I stood at a case waiting for help and when the employee saw me, he literally rolled his eyes. In the other store, you are always greeted, people seem happy, and they even insist on taking your groceries to the car for you. I asked advice of one of the people behind the meat counter one day and he came out from behind the counter and led me to an aisle where we discussed ingredients for a recipe. Where would you rather shop?

Looking for characteristics in a good CSR? Here are a few you might consider:

- I love to serve people.
- I get personal satisfaction from helping others.
- I take pride in my job.
- I hold myself accountable for outcomes.
- I take ownership of results.
- My goal is to make the Customer smile.

---

[8] Gallo, Carmine. "How Southwest And Virgin America Win By Putting People Before Profit." Forbes. September 10, 2013.

Factor 4—There is no direct link between treating a Customer to an Extra Scoop experience and the benefit they receive for doing so.

Yes, it is the CSRs' job to provide good service and yes, you are paying them to do that job. However, it is vitally important to openly paint the picture of what their good work means for them and it has to be something more than "you get to keep your job." You must create a link from creating the Extra Scoop experience and the reward. This, of course, is known as creating an incentive. Let's take that a step further.

One of my favorite business authors is Verne Harnish (which you may have guessed, given he wrote the foreword). If you haven't read his book *Mastering the Rockefeller Habits*, you should pause what you are doing and order it. Chapter Six of that book is all about quarterly themes, and one very important aspect of the quarterly theme is the scoreboard.

About twenty-five years ago, a particularly small player in a very large US industry got written up in *Businessweek* because of their service center. What did they do differently? A lot of things, but primarily, they rewarded Customer Service employees for the activities that resulted in great Customer Service. Things like positive survey scores, average wait time on phones, etc. were tracked. On a very large scoreboard in the lobby, they had each category and metric with two columns. Column one was for the target score for that particular metric and column two was for the actual result for *that day*! If the target was hit, x dollars went into a big pot. The scoreboard also showed how much was contributed to the pot that day and what the accumulation was for the quarter to date. At the end of each quarter, the money was distributed according to a well-publicized formula to the CSRs.

Scoreboards can be very powerful. They remove uncertainty in the target audience's mission and instill trust. They provide immediate feedback of successes and failures to the team. Score-boards are omnipresent, always reminding the team of their goals. Finally, the time distance between behavior and reward is visceral. Simply put, it creates an incentive, a tracking mechanism, and report card in one place.

People, adding an Extra Scoop is quite sensible. Don't you agree?

Your Chapter 8 Extra Scoop
Be so good at Customer Service that any employee might be perceived as the owner.

PART III

Now What?

CHAPTER 9

Let's Get Ready!

What we have walked through in this book are the building blocks of good Customer Service. If you do them all well, you can have great Customer Service. For many of you, they will be a repeat of what you've learned at other times in your career but perhaps have forgotten over the years. And for some, it will be the first time hearing them. I am particularly excited for these building blocks to good Customer Service because they can radically change your organization.

Some of you may be thinking, "This doesn't apply to us. We don't offshore our service teams." Others might be thinking, "This is all for the big guys." For all of you thinking you cannot improve your Customer Service, let me challenge you and say yes, you can.

By the way, just because an aspect of Customer Service didn't appear in this book doesn't mean it isn't an important area to consider. Perhaps it is even unique to your business. Therefore, I further challenge you to identify those areas and make them better. The contents of this book were not meant to be exhaustive—so go ahead and create your own Extra Scoops too! Get your team around the table and ask the question, "Whatever happened to _____?" Don't settle. Be better than your competition. If you look deep enough, you can find ways to make improvements, and those improvements can create massive positive change.

IPEM

Our strategy for improving Customer Service can be implemented in four key stages:

1) Identify: Look deep and determine the areas that need to be aggressively pursued for improvement.
2) Plan: Develop the overall strategy for improving the area(s).
3) Execute: Execute the plan.
4) Measure: Measure for the plan for success.

We will look at these stages individually, but let's do some preparation first.

GETTING READY

*Give me six hours to chop down a tree and I will spend
the first four sharpening the axe.*
—Abraham Lincoln

Every well-executed strategy begins with preparation. Here's some ideas on getting ready to tackle your Customer Service deficiencies:

1) **Lead.** Go all in. Some of you already embrace the need and desire to be great at Customer Service and you will need to make some tweaks. For others, you will need to break up the very foundation

of how you view Customer Service. Take the leap and be willing to do what doesn't feel natural. You are going to have to truly expose yourself, your team, and the organization. You have to be all in, or you're not in. If you want to be Extra-Scoop Certified, then you *have* to be all in. If you do stick with it, and you're willing to genuinely and objectively look at your Customer Service delivery and all the nasty, scary stuff that may be there, you will be on your way to separating yourself form the competition.

2) **Identify the improvement teams.** Make this fun and engaging. Call the improvement team something motivating like the "Customer SWAT Team" or the "Customer Avengers" (I am quite partial to Captain America myself). Whatever you call it, the core mission is Customer Service improvement. You are going to want people who are willing to step up and speak, and you want them from various areas of the organization. You will set up the team and organization for failure if you put all the same people in the room who meet regularly around a conference table and turn a blind eye to Customer Service. Most importantly, you want some people who are on the front lines every day. They will certainly know where the problems are and many of the Scoops that are missing.

   i) You may also want to include representatives from IT, product development, sales, production, and other departments. In some companies with certain product or service offerings, such representatives may need to be permanent members. For the Customer Service professionals you place on the team, I would suggest limiting their participation to a set period of time, like three or six months as an example. It's important to gain fresh perspectives from the front lines and this will also help get more people engaged in the program faster—right in the seats where it counts most. Keep in mind that the people who you engage to identify the challenges may not be the same people who you use on the team for implementation. In fact, I suggest these be two separate teams with two separate charters. Having the "doers" in the room may slow down identification of real problems, as they provide friction with "how will we ever change that?" attitudes. The team you assemble to identify issues must be unhindered and free to tear all the covers off. Your implementation team should have "make it happen" mindsets with the necessary tools, whether it is a sledge hammer or small screwdriver, to put a plan into action. Identify this team after you have identified all the Customer Service problems that need to be addressed. After all, you don't go to a specialized doctor until you determine the root of the problem.

3) **Set a meeting rhythm.** As you have now read in Verne Harnish's book (you did run right out and buy a copy, didn't you?), setting a meeting rhythm is absolutely vital. You should have at least a quick daily huddle by this team—it can be quick and to the point—and longer meeting sessions to tackle

the big stuff (like the first meetings to identify areas of opportunity). Expect the "big stuff" meetings to be longer and more frequent at first, then taper off over time. For now, just be ready to meet regularly.

4) **Study what works—together.** There are many texts on the subject besides this one (I have even mentioned some). Read them. Visit your industry peers. What is Customer Service like with them? What do they do differently and more effectively? Bring in consultants. Find people better than you and immerse yourself and your team. Key point: bringing in outside people should in no way be used as a shortcut to the IPEM strategy, but rather just a tool in the process. Shortcuts will derail your plan and make it more difficult to create buy-in.

5) **Get the team on the same page.** You will need some common reference points and frame setting to get the juices going. Start with this question: "The mission of any Customer Service team should be
_____." You are going to get a lot of answers, but it will be helpful to arrive at the only right one. I don't want to give you the answer, but it is in this book and it starts and ends with the letter S and there is an A, an L, and an E in the middle.

6) **Identify measurements and a way to rate aspects of Customer Service.** Do not get caught up in whether or not your measurements account for everything; we just need a place to start. Have the team come up with specific areas they feel should be measured. As you identify problem areas, you can circle back and add to or subtract from the list.

You are going to need an objective scoring system as you start to peel back aspects of Customer Service. Keep this simple at first—you can always come back and refine your scoring system once you identify areas that need attention. Excellent–Adequate–Poor (3–2–1) is pretty straightforward.

Now that we have ourselves ready, it's time to dig in!

Your Chapter 9 Extra Scoop
**Lessons you learn on other people's mistakes are free.
The ones you learn on your own are almost always more expensive.**

CHAPTER 10

Dig In

IDENTIFY

Our goal in this stage is to look deep in the organization and determine just what needs to be fixed. It is improbable that you would need to throw away everything that you do today in Customer Service and start over. As stated previously, however, be prepared for the fact that it might be the very culture of the organization that needs to be addressed. You must submit the whole to examination. You can treat the symptoms but you will never cure your issues without getting to the root of them. As you work through the identification process, be sure to always ask what it is that you do well too. Most people naturally do not want be critical, so it's a good idea to get the things flowing by talking about what you are good at. This will be important to analyze with the rest of the data later. Also, garbage in, garbage out is definitely in play here. Healthy discussions should be generated by the questions below along with those you come up with; that can't happen if everyone is answering yes or no. If that is happening, you have the wrong people in the room or they are afraid of being open and honest, maybe because of another person in the room who should go. Lastly, if you were relying on measurements to determine the effectiveness and quality of your Customer Service to this point, you need to put them away for now. Let's get started.

DNA CHECK

First check the heart of Customer Service—the culture of the company.

1) Does the satisfaction of the Customer appear anywhere in the company mission statement? What about your core values? Your values should reflect your commitment to the Customer.

2) Do you make Customer Service a priority? In what way?

3) Inversely, do you monitor for the regular demonstration of your core values in your Customer Service experience? Are they clearly present?

4) Does everyone understand and believe that they and every other person in the company contribute to your Customer's experience?

5) Starting at the very top, is there buy-in throughout to execute a Customer Service improvement plan?

6) Do you know why your employees leave the company?

7) How is the Customer Service department viewed internally?

8) Do you hold people accountable for the Customer experience as a whole?

9) Do you, at all times, know the number-one Customer Service concern from the Customers' perspective? From the CSRs' perspective?

10) Does the team meet daily to discuss what they are dealing with and to hash through resolutions to those issues?

11) Do you know the very specific service needs of your typical Customer?

What other questions should you be asking?

TACTICAL CHECK

Next, let's look at some very specific areas of Customer Service. Please note again that this list is not meant to be exhaustive, but rather to stimulate your thought processes. There are plenty of ideas within this book and you will hopefully come up with some on your own.

1) How long do people wait to get help?
2) Can a Customer move through your call-routing system within two key presses?
3) Does the Customer have a way to get a human being on the phone quickly? Do you invite them to do it?
4) Is the information a Customer provides via your IVR system immediately available to a CSR?
5) Does the Customer have the option to speak to someone else when they can't understand the CSR?
6) Can a CSR easily escalate a problem?
7) When a problem is escalated, is there a person-to-person hand off?
8) Is there an option to get a real manager on the phone?
9) Is there an opportunity for the Customer to hear about specials, upgrades, or discounts at an appropriate time?
10) Are your CSRs courteous?
11) Do you survey your callers to measure their satisfaction?

12) Do you offer multiple ways for a Customer to connect with your service team?

13) Is there a way I can help myself, like an FAQ section on the website?

14) Do you set and execute upon reasonable expectations for your Customer?

15) Are CSRs empowered to take care of the Customer? In what ways?

16) Is the first goal of your Customer Service process to ultimately make sure your Customer is quickly routed to a person who can *take action* and resolve the Customer's concern?

GATHER EMPIRICAL DATA

We have done some introspection via our questions above; now it's time to go see what is really happening and gain other perspectives.

1) Have the team experience Customer Service for themselves. It may be helpful to do this in pairs — one person to do the "acting" and the other to record what transpires. Call your own support and pretend to be a Customer. Test every possible scenario as is practical. Monitor the areas of measurement you identified in the last chapter and score them with the method the team agreed to. You can also hire a focus group to act as Customers to augment the team's experiences, though I would not substitute the latter for the former.

2) Have managers and executives work side by side or even in place of CSRs. It is important to have the

perspective of the people trying to create a good experience for the Customer. In this scenario, those sitting in the chair must resist the temptation to work in an alternate manner from the people who do it every day. If there is a script in use, then use it. If they must escalate at certain points, then escalate. The idea here is to walk in the shoes of the CSRs. Like number one, it may be a good idea to do this in pairs so someone can be recording observations along the way.

3) Talk to Customers. I strongly recommend that this be as in-person as possible. Surveys are great tools, but they won't replace person-to-person communication. Managers and executives should do the calling (it is a great reputation boost too). People will respond honestly to a manager asking for such feedback about their Customer Service experience. Ask the Customers to articulate some of their favorite things about ANY Customer Service experience they have enjoyed, even if it isn't a competing product or service. Augment this with online surveys and make sure they are succinct. It's one thing to ask me to take time to provide honest feedback, and another to make me spend an hour to give it to you. Also consider offering a little something for the effort; this can be a good time to offer a coupon for the next visit, for example. Naturally, this has the added bonus of soliciting repeat business in the process. An alternate or parallel method for collecting information is sending a postcard. Here are just a few questions you can ask. Don't forget to come up with some on your own:
    i)   How long did you wait on hold before getting help?

ii) Did we meet your expectations?

iii) Was the CSR friendly?

iv) Were you offered the opportunity to upgrade?

v) Is there anything we could have done better?

vi) What other Customer Service experiences have you enjoyed that you would like to see from us?

vii) How likely are you to refer us to another potential Customer?

The last idea for a question is strongly advocated by Fred Reicheld, the inventor of the Net Promoter Score. It is worth researching in the context of improving your Customer Service.

8) Talk to your CSRs. As with item three, this should be in-person and you should be sure to ask about their favorite Customer Service experiences. Ask them what their biggest complaints are. Don't be surprised when you hear that they are frustrated because they cannot affect the outcomes of their service interactions. Likewise, do not be surprised when the most meaningful, actionable items come from this group. Here are a few ideas for them:

i) What do you believe is the *real* current mission of our Customer Service department? Is it ensuring a great experience for everyone? Is it resolving calls as fast as possible?

ii) How do you feel about the Customer Support you deliver?

iii) What is your number-one frustration?

PULL IT ALL TOGETHER

Now that we have gathered a great deal of information, we need to sort and analyze it. What are the common issues you have heard? You should group these together and make note of the frequency and sources. Ask yourself if there are any correlations amongst the issues. For example, do complaints about long wait times have anything to do with IVR problems?

When you are done with this portion of the exercise, you should have identified many of your issues. Mind you, it's possible you didn't catch all of them or that additional issues will come to light as you start to make changes. That is okay. This may need to be an iterative process based on your situation and circumstances. It is also okay if certain issues have only one data point, and don't think that because they do they are any less important than the others. We will prioritize and plan next.

PLAN

CREATING THE SOLUTION MAP

Next, let's take our identified issues and put an attack plan together. Our objective here is to have a solution map that we can execute upon.

First, let's arrange the issues into three categories. Remember, just because an issue appears less than others does not mean it's less important; it may just mean that fewer data sources had the access, insight, or both. Additionally, as you prioritize the identified issues to attack, do not get overwhelmed and do not feel like you need to conquer every facet within the first week. It is okay to slow down and be sure to successfully conquer each issue. In other words, keep the fire hose on one fire until it's under control.

The last thing I will again recommend is that you are sure to review areas that you (or hopefully outsiders) believe you are great at. You may find areas where you are allocating too many resources or focusing too much effort, and these are areas where you may be able to redeploy from. Now, let's get a look at our three categories:

1) **Big Scoops.** These are the important and/or urgent items that need to be addressed right away. They will generally be foundational in nature and/or have been vociferously stated by multiple sources. Examples include core values vacant of positive Customer Service sentiment, inability to get to a human being, and so forth. These items should be tackled first, as they may very well impact other issues in a positive way. These will probably be the most difficult to conquer because they are deep-seated and may require shifts in thought processes.

2) **Spoonfuls.** These may be the largest segments of issues you identify. These will be very important concerns, often tactical in nature, and will be somewhat easier to solve than Big Scoops. Examples include inadequate CRM platforms, complicated ticketing systems, and inefficient handling processes. You will likely see high impact from resolution of these issues, in the area of morale at minimum. One strategy might be to pick one of these to solve while tackling the Big Scoops, as these areas offer quicker (relatively speaking) yet meaningful win opportunities for the team. However, it's important not to delay resolution of the Big Scoops in the process.

3) **Bananas.** These areas for improvement will be low-hanging fruit (get it?). They will be relatively straightforward to solve, but still very important to get to. Some examples might be FAQ creation or providing a toll-free number to call. They may be things that annoy your CSRs and get in the way of doing their job (though those might be Spoonful items, too). Solutions in this area will seem obvious and easy to solve, thus the team will be tempted to tackle them first. Stay on course. Like Spoonfuls, it might be okay to tackle a Banana issue for the sake of some momentum, but it's critical to get the higher-priority items in line.

CREATE THE PLAN

Now we can create our plan of attack. When we are done here, we will have a solution map that can be executed upon.

It is now time for the implementation team to step in. There must be a good transition to the implementation team. The identification team should remain in place as they monitor the implementation team to ensure the solutions and focus do not drift off course from what was actually identified. The implementation team should be tasked with the solution to the specific issues identified, and it is here that we will transition these issues into objectives. They are now goals to be achieved.

It is my belief that there is no one solution that fits all and that each organization and industry has its own unique culture, approaches, and needs. Some issues may be compounding in one organization and not at another, for example. Therefore, it would be difficult to lay out a concise how-to when it comes to fixing every issue identified by every organization. Given the proper time and tools, your team can solve the problems. I will offer that you should encourage the team to think outside of the box. For instance, if you have identified that Customers think you deliver very bad service but you pick up every phone call on the first ring, it is possible that the solution might be to make callers wait a reasonable amount of time longer for help by reallocating resources from answering phones to having more qualified solution specialists to deal with the problems. This is a basic example, but it should make the point: make sure you're considering the big picture with all causes and effects in the identification of solutions.

Your project manager(s) start to play a big role now, as they record actions in whatever medium they might use to track projects and action plans (i.e., a Gantt chart). If you don't have a project manager on staff, that's okay. Just pick a person who is very organized and who you will empower (and they should have no problem being empowered) to keep everyone on track. This person should have "go/no go" and "start/stop" authority. They are the ones who will pull the team back together if something starts to go off course. Incidentally, this should be someone from the managerial ranks versus executive.

A Gantt chart or the like might be more complicated than its worth if you do not have a trained project manager. In that case, simply create a spreadsheet. Your spreadsheet should have time across the top (usually weeks)—as in week one, week two, week three—running left to right. On the left side, running top to bottom, are your identified issues. Under each objective there will be several tasks required to accomplish it. Your spreadsheet will look something like this (please note that the objectives and tasks are just examples and not intended to be comprehensive):

There are a number of objectives that I think should most certainly appear in your solution map if they don't already exist in your organization.

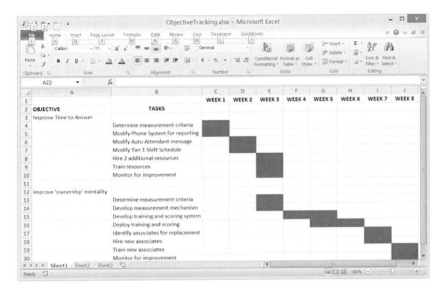

- The first objective in your spreadsheet could be "Change the name of the Customer Service team." This connotes a change in thinking, one where the team will be considered the most vital in the organization. It shows there is a fresh new emphasis on taking care of the Customer. It can be exciting for the team members to be a part of a new initiative. As you did with the implementation and identification groups, make it fun and engaging— inspiring, even. If the new team name puts a smile on your Customer's face, that is even better.

- "Develop protocols and methods for at-risk/un-happy clients." You should create a centralized reporting mechanism and discovery methodology such that the vast majority of the organization can easily communicate if they believe a Customer is not happy or at risk. You might even incent them to do so. The idea is that everyone is on the lookout for an unhappy Customer. You must decide what to do once you have this information. I have seen organizations have departments or individual roles that aggressively work to turn an unhappy/at-risk Customer around. For certain, you should have a concrete plan to address Customers who are unhappy and/or have received a bad experience from your company.

- "Upgrade personnel in the Customer Service team as necessary." Keep in mind that your best people should be in Customer Service, not the ones you don't know what else to do with. We touched on this notion earlier. It is very important that the people in Customer Service are the right people.

- "Establish a morning huddle for CSRs." Have them discuss the number-one issue they are facing, and provide an opportunity for team members to share insights and solutions. This is a great time to remind the team of the metrics that are being tracked and where they stand.

- "Implement a feedback system." There are a number of ways to do this, but you must have a way for Customers to let you know how they feel besides never doing business with you again. It must be easy for them to do.

Now that we have a plan of attack formulated, it's time to go on the offensive.

Your Chapter 10 Extra Scoop
Ask a better question.

CHAPTER 11

Make It Happen

EXECUTE

A great strategy alone won't win a game or a battle;
the win comes from basic blocking and tackling.

—Naveen Jain

Execution of your plan will be the most difficult part of this process, particularly if you have a lot of Big Scoops to tackle. Let me encourage you—your continued growth as a business depends on the team making it happen, so stick with it. You can do it!

Executing upon our solution map seems pretty straightforward, so we will spend a short amount of time on a few key things to keep in mind during the process.

1) This isn't one big fireworks finale. As we identified in our planning stage, there are goals and milestones to be tackled, piece by piece. I feel strongly that an organization, regardless of size, can only absorb so much change at any one time. Moreover, you cannot always correctly anticipate the impact of any particular change, so be deliberate. One of

my favorite sayings is "Do the next right thing." Don't get overwhelmed by all that needs to be done.

2) Use Scoops, not spatulas. This is just my clever way of suggesting to you to make sure your team has the right tools and everything else it needs to make things happen and implement change. Make sure the project manager is fully empowered and is not getting inappropriate resistance. Make sure team members are carrying their weight and not offering roadblocks. If software updates are needed, get them. If new equipment is needed, get it.

3) Have a team huddle every day. Remember that meeting rhythm we have talked about? The implementation team needs to be communicating every day. It doesn't have to be for long—fifteen to thirty minutes should do it. It needs to be long enough to give status, positive progress, and any "stuck in the mud" issues. If anything requires a longer discussion or multiple members, schedule a breakout session. As I have guided you to do prior, be sure to pick up Verne's book for more detail on the daily huddle.

MEASURE

Measure what is measurable, and make measurable what is not so.

—Galileo Galilei

By now, you will hopefully have put forth a tremendous effort to improve your Customer Service. How do you know what impact you have had, and how will you know in the future if things are regressing? Clearly, you must measure key aspects of your delivery, and those key aspects will need to line up with most of the objectives you have identified.

You cannot quantify the success (or failure) of your efforts if you are not measuring the outcomes. Throughout the last few sections and chapters, I have urged you to develop measurements for specific areas of Customer Service, and I hope you have done so. To identify areas to measure, go to each identified objective and ask the question "How can I determine the success of this objective?" You may need to think outside of the box a bit, but you should be able to measure all objectives. If you have stumbled across an objective that you have been unable to determine how or what to measure, then just listen to our friend Galileo and make it measurable. I realize this is easier said than done, but in doing so you may discover fundamental improvements to that particular area or process.

Make sure that information is readily available for tracking purposes; you can't spend hours upon hours gathering data. However, if it is a key area for measurement and you can't easily do so, then one of your objectives should be to get the right tools in place for measurement and tracking. It is key to measure the objectives.

I have included ideas for measurement below. You might get some great ideas for objectives that you did not capture previously just by browsing these ideas. Please note that once again, this list is not intended to be exhaustive. The objectives you have come up with are your own and may even be unique, thus the measurements will be as well.

- Number of repeat Customers
- Top-three complaints by incident count
- Online presence/reputation score

- Total Customer Service incidents
- Customer satisfaction score
- Time to answer
- Average length of call
- Number of second or third calls (alternatively, first-call closes)
- Number of Customer Service requests open
- At-risk identifications
- Customer retention
- Add-on sales/upgrades
- Referrals
- Percent of surveys completed
- Escalation rate
- Employee retention/turnover

Throughout the process, keep a close eye on your measurements and the experiential outcomes. It is sometimes possible that your measurement facilities may not be a true indicator of what is really happening. This will typically happen if you are not measuring the right thing or the measurement system is faulty in some way.

Lastly, make sure that you are advertising the measurements regularly through your daily huddle and especially through the Verne Harnish game board I illustrated back in Chapter 8.

A REAL-LIFE EXAMPLE OF IPEM

Prior to our working together, a longtime Customer of mine was placed in charge of a global IT department. She took it over at a time when there were major issues and dissatisfaction amongst the end users (the Customers). The first thing she did was send out a survey to *identify* the specific issues. She gave out a "token of appreciation" to each user who filled out the survey and received over a 35 percent response rate. She was mortified at the horrible results that came back, hearing things like "we don't even bother to call for help anymore" and "people bite our heads off." With a baseline in hand, she *made a plan* and *executed upon it*. She added new support tools and made staff changes, putting the right people in the right seats or letting them go altogether. She put herself on the front lines and started taking support calls so she knew what her new team was experiencing. Six to eight weeks in, she studied the *measurements* she put in place and the feedback she was now getting from the Customers. One such Customer went out of his way to give her enthusiastic praise, telling her that the changes were quite palpable. He was getting quick responses now and the CSRs were even pleasant to talk to! He thanked her profusely for going above and beyond, though she felt all she did was go *all in* on the job she was assigned. To this day, it bothers her that the expectations for service had become so terribly low before she stepped in.

Adding Extra Scoops with IPEM can have the same results for you. Don't you agree?

Your Chapter 11 Extra Scoop
You must be persistent to achieve a goal, but you must be consistent to maintain it.

CHAPTER 12

Wrap Up

People don't buy what you do; they buy why you do it.

—Simon Sinek

I would expect that at some point in your career, you have seen the below Customer declarations. I think they are worth noting within this book, since mindset is so critical when it comes to Customer Service. If I am responsible for Customer Service, I want all of my people to believe in these declarations. I want them to be passionate about them—they are part of the "why" for me.

The text below is credited to Kenneth B. Elliott from a 1941 interview.[9] Elliott worked for the Studebaker Corporation, but what is more remarkable was his role: he was the vice president in charge of SALES. Isn't it interesting that an executive responsible for sales communicated this sentiment?

It is, of course, not possible to state with any practical exactitude what the Customer is. But there are several common denominators to be found

---

[9] "The Customer is Not an Interruption in Our Work; He Is the Purpose of It." Quote Investigator. August 2, 2012.

when we consider the Customer in terms of what he is not. These things, I think, are fundamental to intelligent Customer relationship and, it may be added, most of them apply pretty well to the vast majority of prospects as well.

1) The Customer is not dependent upon us— we are dependent upon him.
2) The Customer is not an interruption of our work—he is the purpose of it.
3) The Customer is not a rank outsider to our business—he is a part of it.
4) The Customer is not a statistic—he is a flesh-and-blood human being completely equipped with biases, prejudices, emotions, pulse, blood chemistry, and possibly a deficiency of certain vitamins.
5) The Customer is not someone to argue with or match wits against—he is a person who brings us his wants. If we have sufficient imagination, we will endeavor to handle them profitably to him and to ourselves.

A FEW LAST POINTS TO REMEMBER

- I have said many times that you can create a truly memorable Customer experience two ways: by exceeding expectations or by failing to meet them. There is nothing in between. Think about that for a moment. What memorable experiences are you providing?
- If the status quo for your organization is "just okay" Customer Service, then challenge it.

- Even if you only implement one or two changes that you have been so inspired to accomplish, you could set into motion great momentum for positive change and make a great impact on the team, your company, and maybe even your industry. Maybe your industry needs you!

- You won't always do it perfectly, but you can always do it right. What does that mean? It means that while you may make mistakes along the way, you can always do it with the right passion and purpose.

ONE LAST ICE-CREAM STORY

As I reached my teenage years, my grandparents retired back to Alabama, where I used to spend summers with them. One day my grandfather suggested we go buy an electric ice-cream maker and make ice cream. I could not think of a more fun thing to do to beat the heat and humidity of summer day in Alabama. We bought the ice-cream maker and went into the boathouse to actually start the process. As I remember it, we ran into a problem almost immediately, as the maker kept freezing up and not rotating properly. My grandfather moved the maker into the sun to help melt some of the ingredients and restore the maker to operation. My job was to stand by the outlet where it was plugged in and plug or unplug the unit at his command as he wrestled the mixer forward and back to loosen it. "Unplug it. Okay, plug it in. Unplug it. Plug it back in." This went on for about twenty minutes. I am not the most patient person these days, but you should have seen me as a teenager. I let out a loud sigh of frustration to which my grandfather "politely" suggested we trade places and I stand in the sun and mess around with the maker while he stood in the shade and did the plug pulling. As I passed him to take over his post he said, "This is going to be great ice cream, we just need to be patient and put in a little effort. That's usually when the best things come to us."

You might think this contrived, but I promise you it is a true story. We eventually were able to get ice cream out of that thing and he was right—it was great. Naturally, there is a moral to all of this. Getting your ice cream—er, your Customer Service—running on all cylinders may not be an easy task, but it will certainly be worth it when you make it happen.

Your Chapter 12 Extra Scoop
"The starting point of all achievement is desire."
—Napoleon Hill

ABOUT THE AUTHOR

John Mamon has been a leader in the IT service industry for over twenty years. He has partnered to grow and sell one of the most successful managed-services providers (MSPs) in the Atlanta area and currently is the president and CEO of another MSP, mPowered IT. mPowered IT's number-one core value is "to provide a great experience to everyone we interact with." John has led multiple facets of organizations including sales, service delivery, and operations, and lives in the Atlanta area with his wife, Christine, and two daughters, Samantha and Alexis.

For more great Extra Scoop information, please visit John's website at www.extrascoops.com or contact him at info@ExtraScoops.com.

Did you come up with a great way to enhance your Customer Service delivery? Do you have a success to report? Help us all be better and let us know on Twitter @ShareExtraScoops.

Are you a Customer? Got an Extra Scoop experience to report (good) or did your Scoop hit the floor (bad)? Tell us your Customer Service stories @MyExtraScoop.